ARCHITECT OF BECOMING

From Proving to Being

Lauren Thompson

Published by Freiling Agency
Hilton Head Island, South Carolina
www.FreilingAgency.com

PB ISBN: 978-1-969826-57-3
HB ISBN: 978-1-969826-59-7
E-Book ISBN: 978-1-969826-58-0

Contents

Introduction

This is not the book I thought I would write.

For years, when I imagined writing about leadership, I envisioned something very different. A book about strategy, perhaps. Or organizational systems. Or the technical aspects of health policy and information technology that occupied my professional life for decades. Something analytical, well-researched, properly footnoted. Something that demonstrated expertise and competence and mastery.

Something safe.

Instead, I find myself writing about the messiest parts of being human—about feelings. Feeling like I never quite belonged, about striving for perfection while always feeling inadequate, about chronic illness and solo parenting and burnout so severe it required years to recover from. About breaking down completely before I could be rebuilt differently. About all the ways I got it wrong before I began to understand what actually mattered.

This is a book about leadership, but not in the way you might expect. It's not about climbing the corporate ladder or achieving executive positions or implementing strategic frameworks—though all of that is in here. It's about a different kind of leadership: the leadership of becoming authentically yourself, of serving something larger than your own ambition, of developing the capacity to hold complexity and paradox, of learning to trust emergence rather than control everything.

It's a book about what happens when the path you think you're supposed to follow leads you somewhere entirely unexpected. When the life you carefully planned falls apart. When the identity you built over decades crumbles. When you have to start over, not knowing who you'll become in the rebuilding.

The story I tell in these pages spans more than forty years—from a premature birth that shaped my nervous system in ways I wouldn't understand until middle age, through a career navigating male-dominated organizations and the complex intersection of healthcare policy and technology, to the decision to adopt a child as a single woman in my forties, to multiple encounters with burnout and chronic illness, to an eventual transformation I never could have predicted or planned.

It's the story of being the black sheep—the middle child who never quite fit, the woman who approached things differently, the leader whose style wasn't understood or valued in conventional organizational hierarchies. For most of my life, I experienced being different as a problem to be solved, evidence that something was wrong with me. It took decades and considerable suffering to understand that being different wasn't a flaw but a feature, not a weakness but a potential gift—if I could learn to honor it rather than fight it.

This is also a love story—about the unexpected, transformative love of mothering an adopted son with significant learning differences, about what it means to advocate for a child who sees and experiences the world differently, about how parenting taught me more about leadership than any doctoral program or executive role ever could.

And it's a cautionary tale about the price of perfectionism, about what happens when you spend decades trying to prove you're enough by achieving more, doing more, being more—until your body rebels with chromosomal mutations and your psyche collapses under the weight of impossible expectations. About the breaking points we hit when we refuse to acknowledge our limits. About what resilience actually means, which is not the same as endurance.

But ultimately, this is a book about transformation. About the journey from "not enough" to "already whole." From control to trust. From proving to being. From individual achievement to collective service. From seeing leadership as position and power to understanding it as consciousness and capacity. From believing you can plan your way through life to learning to trust what emerges.

I didn't choose this path. It chose me, often through experiences I would never have chosen for myself—loss and illness and failure and breakdown. But those experiences, as difficult as they were to live through, taught me things I couldn't have learned any other way. They broke me open to wisdom that was always there but that I couldn't access while I was armored in achievement and expertise.

The chapters that follow trace this journey chronologically, but they also trace a developmental arc—from earlier stages of making meaning to more complex, integrated ways of being in the world. If you're familiar with adult development theory, you'll recognize the progression from conventional to post-conventional consciousness. If you're not, don't worry—I'll explain what you need to know as you learn along the way.

What I hope you'll find in these pages is not just my story but something of your own story as well. Because while the specifics are mine—the premature birth, the adoption, the particular career path, the chronic myeloid leukemia—the underlying patterns are universal.

The feeling of not belonging. The drive to prove yourself. The perfectionism that looks like strength but is actually fear. The crisis that forces you to question everything. The descent into darkness that precedes transformation. The slow, difficult work of rebuilding yourself differently. The discovery that who you're becoming is more important than what you're achieving.

These are human experiences, leadership experiences, development experiences. And if you've lived long enough and honestly enough, you've encountered some version of them too.

I'm not writing this book as someone who has it all figured out. I'm writing as someone still in process, still becoming, still learning. The journey doesn't end with recovery and reinvention. It continues, always continues, with new challenges and new opportunities for growth.

But I'm writing from a different place than where I started. From greater spaciousness. From more compassion—for myself and others. From understanding that being human means being flawed and limited and messy, and that embracing that reality rather than fighting it is where real strength and wisdom emerge.

I'm writing because I believe that sharing our struggles—not just our successes—is how we help each other. That vulnerability is not weakness but courage. That the stories we're most afraid to tell are often the ones most worth telling.

And I'm writing because I've learned something crucial about leadership that I wish I had understood decades ago: that the most important leadership is the leadership of your own life. That before you can lead others effectively, you need to know yourself deeply. That authentic leadership flows from being fully yourself rather than performing a role or meeting others' expectations.

This is the wisdom I've gained from the unexpected path. And if it helps you navigate your own unexpected path—if it gives you permission to honor your differences, to trust your journey, to embrace your struggles as teachers, to let go of perfection and control—then perhaps all of it, even the hardest parts, will have served a purpose larger than my own development.

The path continues. For me, for you, for all of us learning to be more conscious, more capable, more compassionate human beings and leaders.

Let's walk it together.

CHAPTER 1

The Black Sheep Awakens

The summers of my childhood smelled like salt air and sunscreen, tasted like fresh-caught lobster split open on newspaper spread across a weathered picnic table. On Block Island, my father would surface from the blue-green water with his spearfishing catch while my mother watched from the beach, perpetually worried he'd been down too long. My sister Caryn, my brother Brian, and I would body surf until our lips turned purple, then sprawl on towels, sun-drunk and happy, while the adults talked and laughed in canvas chairs that sank into the sand.

These are the memories I return to when I think of my early years: love, laughter, adventure. Summer evenings in our Connecticut backyard playing badminton and croquet, and weekends sailing on Long Island Sound. Winter weekends careening down ski slopes in Vermont, then a week each year in a cabin that smelled of wood smoke and wet wool. Our street is alive with neighborhood kids playing kickball until dark, then capturing the flag with flashlights cutting through the humid summer nights. The ferry ride from Narragansett to Block Island, standing at the rail with my siblings, racing to spot the island first.

My memories of early childhood are unambiguously happy ones. And yet.

There was always something else. A feeling I couldn't name then, that I'm only now beginning to fully understand. A sense of being slightly out of step, watching from just outside the frame of the family portrait even as I stood squarely within it.

Heritage and Foundation

The characteristics that defined our family ran deep, carried across oceans and centuries: independence, stubbornness, intelligence. These traits pervaded our home like the smell of my dad's pipe tobacco, like the sound of my mother's laugh—inescapable, foundational, shaping everything that grew within their influence.

My mother, Virginia (Ginny to those who knew her) was the fourth child and only daughter of immigrants who fled what is now Belarus and Poland during the Russian Revolution of 1917. They settled in the small Connecticut town of Branford, where my grandfather operated a tailor shop and dry cleaning business. Virginia inherited her parents' intelligence and fierce independence. After high school, she worked as a secretary at Southern New England Telephone Company, where she had a promising career ahead of her. She gave it up to raise her family—a common choice for women of her generation, but one I suspect cost her more than she ever said aloud. Years later, she returned to work and eventually completed her college degree. The year she graduated, one year after I did, I couldn't have been more proud. She had shown me something essential: it's never too late to reclaim the path you set aside.

My father, George (also known as Beans),, carried his own immigrant legacy. His father, George V., came from Scotland by way of Canada and settled in New Haven, where he worked as a railroad engineer. He married Louisa, a descendant of Mayflower families who had settled in Massachusetts generations earlier. Dad was a talented student and swimmer in high school, skills that served him well during his four years in the Navy as a signal communications specialist. After his service, he completed his bachelor's degree at Northeastern University in Boston, then entered the emerging field of computing—a decision that would place him at the leading edge of a technological revolution.

He cut his teeth at Bell Labs in New Jersey, working in information theory and systems analysis, contributing to the development of early computer and telecommunications systems. Later, back in Connecticut with New Haven Telephone Company, where he spent the remainder of his career, he was known as a highly skilled analyst and engineer. His legacy lives on in the design of the computer center he helped create.

My parents met on Block Island—that magical place that would become woven through the fabric of my entire life. When they married, they settled in Connecticut and designed a contemporary ranch-style house in Branford, full of modern features unusual for homes of that era. Even in this choice, their independence and forward-thinking nature showed through. They built a life together that valued intellectual curiosity, education, and the kind of scientific thinking that sees the world as something to be understood, decoded, investigated.

All three of their surviving children—myself, my sister, and my brother—would pursue careers in scientific fields. It was simply what you did in our family: you asked questions, you sought answers, you learned. I remember coming home from elementary school with my arms full of library books, adding them to the stacks already piling up beside my bed. We were always reading something. This love of learning, instilled so early and so thoroughly, would become the throughline of my entire life—the one constant as everything else shifted and transformed.

The Shadow at the Beginning

But before I could read those books, before I could ask those questions, I had to survive.

I was born six weeks premature, the middle child between Caryn, who was a year and a half older, and Brian, who would arrive three years after me. Before Caryn, there had been another child, a miscarriage that my mother carried with her always, a presence that shaped our family in ways we children never fully understood.

Those six weeks I spent in an incubator, separated from my mother's touch by necessity and medical technology, were touch and go. The doctors weren't certain I would make it. But I did. I survived, breathing on my own, growing strong enough to finally go home.

I am only now, decades later, fully appreciating what those early weeks did to me. How they shaped the neural pathways forming in my premature brain. How the absence of my mother's heartbeat, her warmth, her smell—all the things a newborn expects and needs—created patterns I would spend a lifetime unconsciously following.

And I've begun to think, too, about what that time must have been like for my sister Caryn. One and a half years old, suddenly without her mother's full attention, her parents were consumed with worry over a baby she couldn't see, couldn't touch, who existed somewhere in a hospital behind glass. What patterns were being formed in her brain during those weeks? How did my precarious entrance into the world shape the sibling dynamics that would define so much of both our childhoods?

While I was surrounded by love—and I was, genuinely and completely—I always felt a bit different from my siblings. Some of this may be classic middle child syndrome, that peculiar position of being neither the trailblazing firstborn nor the coddled baby of the family. But it was more than that.

I experienced things differently. I reacted differently. And increasingly as I grew, I felt I always had to prove myself, that I was never quite good enough. There was a persistent sense of not being noticed, a feeling that would pervade my adult life and career in ways I'm still unraveling.

Most acutely, I lived in the shadow of my older, smarter, more athletically talented sister.

This became particularly prominent when I entered high school. With each new year, each new class, I heard the same question: "Are you Caryn's sister?" Teachers, coaches, other students—everyone had known Caryn first. "You must be Caryn's sister," they would say, with the implicit expectation that I was just like her.

I was not.

We are, in fact, quite different people. But how do you establish your own identity when everyone is looking for someone else's reflection in your face?

This place in my family—the middle, the different one, the black sheep—made me a little more rebellious. I think I tested the will of my parents on many occasions, pushing boundaries they hadn't needed to defend with Caryn, asserting myself in ways that must have been exhausting for them.

But it also gave me something valuable. It developed in me the skills of a mediator, a diplomat. Throughout my personal life and career, I have found myself in this role again and again: the one who sees both sides, who can translate between conflicting parties, who can find the middle ground. Middle children are known for being highly empathetic and persuasive, often trailblazers as they carve out their own path. We're drawn to social causes, to helping, to making things better.

All of these became part of my being. They would fuel my quest to do good, to save the world, to help others along the way. My later career in health policy and leadership coaching followed in lockstep with these early-formed motivations, though I couldn't have predicted that path from where I stood as a teenager, still trying to answer the question: "Who are you, if not Caryn's sister?"

The Quirky Empath

I've always been a little quirky. I needed to be my own person, even as I desperately wanted to belong. I wanted to be part of the group, yet I needed to separate myself, to be different. These contradictory impulses took me on the life path that eventually emerged—not the one I might have planned, but the one that was somehow always waiting for me.

I've always been an empath, connected with others in a way not everyone experiences. I feel things deeply, often taking on the emotions of those around me like a radio picking up signals I can't turn off. I've always had an ability to sense things others can't—shifts in energy, unspoken tensions, the truth beneath the words people say. I didn't come to appreciate this ability until adulthood, and even now I'm still learning to understand it, to work with it rather than being overwhelmed by it.

This awareness, both known and unknown, has transcended my life—influencing paths taken and not taken, decisions made and unmade. It has taken me a lifetime to know myself in this way.

When I studied the Enneagram a few years ago, much of my nature and my instincts began to come into focus. I could see the patterns that had shaped me as a child and followed me into adulthood. I could name the things I had always felt but never understood. My journey of self-discovery, I began to understand just how much my early life created the foundation of who I was and who I would become

But even that wasn't the full picture.

I learned much later in life—really, just in the last few years—how much my need to chart my own course is grounded in those earliest experiences: my premature birth, those six weeks in an incubator, the way I entered the world fighting for each breath.

Patterns are established very early in our lives, without our awareness or knowledge. They embed themselves in our brains, in the neural pathways, in our very being. The brain of a premature infant, developing outside the womb in an environment of bright lights and medical equipment rather than the dark warmth of the mother's body, forms different connections. The nervous system learns different lessons about safety and threat, connection and isolation.

These patterns are sometimes hard to recognize unless you're looking for them. And they are definitely hard to change.

I began to study the neuroscience of birth and childhood trauma when I adopted my son as an infant—a child who had his own traumatic birth experience. I was trying to understand him, to help him, to know how to mother a child whose early experiences had shaped his brain in ways that would affect him for life.

But in studying his story, my own life began to come into focus.

I began to understand how my experiences as a child influenced my entire life trajectory and career. The feeling of being separate, of watching from outside, of needing to prove myself—these weren't character flaws or personality quirks. They were adaptive responses, neural patterns formed in those critical early weeks and reinforced throughout my childhood.

The black sheep wasn't broken. The black sheep was simply wired differently.

In keeping with my lifelong need for knowledge and mastery, I dove into this new quest for understanding. I read about polyvagal theory, about attachment styles, about the developing brain. I learned about how trauma—even preverbal trauma, trauma that lives in the body rather than in memory—shapes everything that comes after.

And I learned something else: that understanding these patterns doesn't erase them, but it does transform them. What once felt like evidence of not being enough became the foundation for a different kind of strength. The ability to sense what others miss, to mediate between competing needs, to chart my own course even when it's uncomfortable—these grew from the same roots as my feelings of inadequacy.

The black sheep was awakening to her own nature. Not as a problem to be solved, but as a gift to be understood and ultimately shared with others walking their own difficult paths.

Seeds of Everything to Come

Those summer evenings in our Connecticut backyard, the ferry rides to Block Island, my father emerging from the water with his catch, my arms full of library books—these remain true and precious memories. The love was real. The happiness was real.

And the feeling of being different was also real.

Both things can be true at once. That's something it took me decades to understand.

The premature infant in the incubator was already learning the lessons that would define her life: that survival requires fighting, that connection is precious because it can be interrupted, that the world is a place to be figured out and mastered because understanding brings safety.

The middle child was learning her own lessons: that identity must be claimed rather than given, that seeing all sides is both a gift and a burden, that helping others can be a way of helping yourself.

The black sheep was learning the most important lesson of all: that being different isn't a failure of fitting in. It's an invitation to become something else entirely.

I couldn't have articulated any of this as a child. I lived it without understanding it, felt it without naming it. The neural pathways were being laid down, the patterns were forming, and I was becoming the person I would spend the rest of my life learning to know.

The quest for understanding—of the world, of others, of myself—had begun. It would take me through education and career, through adoption and motherhood, through chronic illness and burnout and reinvention. It would take me to the breaking point and beyond it, to a place where all these early experiences would finally converge into something like wisdom.

But that journey was still ahead. For now, there was just a girl who felt things deeply, who read voraciously, who loved her family and felt separate from them all at once. A girl who would carry these contradictions forward into a life neither she nor anyone else could have predicted.

The black sheep was awakening. But she didn't yet know where she was being called to go.

CHAPTER 2

The Quest for Understanding

I have always lived primarily in my head. Ideas fascinate me more than small talk. Theories draw me deeper than gossip. Give me a complex problem to solve, a pattern to decode, a system to understand, and I am fully alive. Put me in a room full of people making conversation about nothing in particular, and I am quietly calculating my escape route.

This is who I have always been: the girl with her nose in a book, the teenager who would rather read about neuroscience than go to parties, the woman who finds organizational systems as compelling as other people find reality television. I learned much later that this tendency to prioritize ideas and thoughts over people is characteristic of my personality type—a defining feature, not a failing. But in my youth, it simply felt like another way I was different, another reason I didn't quite fit.

The foundations of who I would become—my personal drive, my intellectual curiosity, my deep desire to effect positive change—began to crystallize during my educational journey. But the path was neither straight nor easy. And the quest for understanding that would define my entire life began with trying to understand how to simply be good enough.

High School: The Studious Introvert

My journey through high school was more or less uneventful, at least on the surface. Aside from a rebellious period in my middle teens—testing boundaries, pushing back against expectations, asserting myself as someone other than "Caryn's sister"—I was generally the studious type. I didn't socialize much. Being an introvert and somewhat on the nerdy side, my social life was subdued at best. There were parties here and there, most of which I didn't enjoy. I was shy and reserved, sometimes socially awkward, qualities that would follow me into later personal and work relationships. But, I discovered the joys of running and cycling, being outside, connecting with my body, and the recuperative power of being with nature.

But my rebellious side never fully disappeared. It would show up regularly throughout my life and career, though not in obvious ways. It generally took the form of a need to be different, to not accept the status quo for what it was. I was always looking for a new and better way, always searching for paths around roadblocks. This often left me outside the spheres of influence I both longed for and stood apart from. Over time, I stopped seeing this as a problem and began wearing it as a badge of honor. The black sheep doesn't follow the flock.

When it came time to apply for college, I was certain of two things. One: I wanted to be away from home. Two: I didn't want to go to the same school as my sister.

This was my chance to finally separate myself from the overwhelming influence of Caryn's shadow, to spread my wings and discover who I might be when no one was comparing me to someone else. With my passion for science and deep interest in biology, I chose Colgate University. Like most kids heading to college and away from home for the first time, I was terrified and excited in equal measure. I was anxious to continue my education, make new friends, and begin what I thought of as my real life journey.

College, it turned out, was a shock to my system.

Everything that had worked for me before stopped working. My straight A's from high school transformed into B's and C's in college, and the impact on my self-esteem was devastating. The things I had always relied on—my intellect, my ability to put in the time, my dedication to studying—weren't cutting it at this level. I studied most of the time when I wasn't working, yet I could never get ahead of the imposing workload. I also began to discover the social side of myself. I would be drawn into a circle of friends who I could let down my guard with and share a part of me that mostly stays hidden away from others.

I always studied alone. It was the only way I knew how, the only way that seemed to work for me. I would learn later that this is a defining characteristic of introverts—a trait deeply ingrained in my being. While my extroverted classmates formed study groups and learned together, I holed up in the library by myself, trying to absorb everything through sheer force of will.

It wasn't enough. And once again, I felt like I wasn't enough.

Working My Way Through

To this day, I am grateful and indebted to my parents, who worked to finance my education. I was fortunate to have some scholarship and work-study financing that made Colgate possible. I wouldn't fully appreciate until much later the sacrifices my parents made for me and my siblings so we could attend the schools of our choice.

I was among the work-study crowd. My first job was meal service in the cafeteria—serving food, clearing trays, scrubbing industrial-sized pots in the steamy dishroom. I moved on to the library front desk, stamping due dates and reshelfing books. Eventually, I landed what was probably the best work-study position on campus: manning the beer fountain at the campus pub.

All three jobs were memorable and led to many friendships. As you might imagine, the pub was the most fun. Through these experiences, I learned to juggle school and work—a skill that would serve me well throughout my life, though at the time it felt more like barely keeping my head above water.

I took on some club sports during college: rugby and rowing. Why rugby and rowing? Perhaps it was my desire to be different, my need to stand apart. These were not mainstream sports, not the expected choices. They were hard, physical, demanding—and somehow that appealed to me.

I also continued to run. Unlike team sports, running I preferred to do alone. It became my time for thoughts and dreams, my escape into—and sometimes from—the constant churning of my own mind. I live in my head, and running and cycling became portals to a different kind of consciousness. They gave me a window into the mind-body connection, which would later become a way for me to ground and center myself during stressful and challenging times.

Through running, I learned to manage my thoughts and emotions. The rhythm of feet hitting pavement, breath synchronized with movement, the physical exhaustion that finally quieted the relentless thinking—exercise became a way of life, a daily ritual. At times, it became a crutch, a way to run from feelings I didn't want to face. But mostly, it was medicine.

I had carried to college my need to escape into nature during times of stress, whenever I needed to reconnect with myself. Walking in the woods, sitting by the water—these gave me a sense of peace and connection with something outside of myself. It would be much later in life when I came to fully appreciate what I was doing. As I began to delve into mindfulness and meditation, I realized these had always been my ways of calming my mind and grounding myself. These habits continue to anchor me, to keep me centered when everything else is spinning.

The Medical School Dream

Some things remained constant through my college years: my intense interest in science and my need to prove myself. At one point, I thought I would pursue medicine as a career. I imagined myself as a doctor, healing people, making a tangible difference in individual lives.

But when I realized that probably wasn't in the cards—my grades would never get me into medical school—I found myself in a quandary. What did I want to do with my life? What did I want to be when I grew up?

The question haunted me. I spent hours poring over career resources in the library, reading about different fields, trying to find something that would ignite the same passion that medicine once had. Eventually, I leaned into healthcare management. I knew I wanted to be in a field where I could help people and have an impact on the world. If I couldn't heal individuals directly, perhaps I could heal systems.

I'm fascinated with science and behavior. Particularly the human body and the human brain—how neurons fire, how memories form, how consciousness emerges from electrical impulses and chemical reactions. It seems almost miraculous that we function as well as we do given the sheer complexity of our anatomy and physiology.

And I'm equally fascinated with organizations. Collections of people, each with their own personalities, behaviors, and tendencies, interacting on formal and informal levels, driven by multitudes of motivations and desires. Organizations, I came to understand, have many similarities to the human body and brain. They are complex adaptive systems, operating according to principles that mirror chaos theory—small changes cascading into large effects, patterns emerging from apparent randomness, order and disorder dancing together.

These ideas and fascinations would come together in the career path I eventually chose. The themes emerged frequently and regularly throughout my education and career, driving my decision to pursue the intersection of health policy and management, strategic management and information technology.

This path was not explicitly planned. It emerged over time as I pursued opportunities that came along in areas that interested me and that felt impactful. I was following a pattern I couldn't yet see, responding to pulls I didn't fully understand. The black sheep was finding her way, even if she couldn't articulate the destination.

Understanding the INTJ

Years later, in my quest to know myself,, I would learn about the Myers-Briggs Type Indicator and discover I fit the INTJ personality type to a tee, which is also known as the intuitive introvert.

INTJs are Introverted, Intuitive, Thinking, Judging types—strategists with a deep thirst for knowledge. We prefer to work and make decisions alone. We are private, independent, logical, organized, and quiet. We are creative and tend to look at the big picture rather than getting lost in details. We see patterns and possibilities. We are often more comfortable with theoretical discussions than with small talk, and we may appear aloof to people who don't understand us.

We are driven by competence and mastery. We value self-improvement obsessively. We question conventional wisdom as a matter of course, always looking for better ways, more efficient systems, deeper understanding.

How did the test know this about me? It felt like someone had written my biography in bullet points.

Understanding this about myself—that I wasn't broken or strange, just wired differently—would have helped during those difficult college years. But perhaps I needed to struggle through the confusion first, to feel the inadequacy deeply, before I could appreciate the gifts that came with my particular neural architecture.

The Job Hunt and the Working World

The year I graduated from college was not a great year in the job market. I remember spending hours at my parents' house writing innumerable cover letters and sending out resumes—to jobs I was barely qualified for and many that I was overqualified for—hoping someone would recognize my potential beneath my unremarkable GPA.

Months went by. Finally, a job came through. It was not my dream job, but it would pay the bills until I figured out my next move. I moved to Boston to live with one of my college roommates and entered the working world.

Boston was a great place to be as a recent college graduate—vibrant, full of young people, offering just enough independence while still feeling manageable. I was learning to spread my wings a little further beyond the protective shield of college, testing what it meant to be an adult in the real world.

But after a while, my desire to learn and do more than I was doing took hold. It always did. I couldn't simply coast, couldn't be satisfied with good enough. I applied to graduate school and was accepted to The George Washington University to pursue a master's degree in healthcare management and policy.

Moving to Washington, DC felt like the beginning of something significant. A new city, new friends, new challenges, a lot of learning—though still without a clear sense of what I wanted to do with this new degree once I earned it.

Not wanting to be on a traditional hospital track requiring a year-long residency, I opted for a shorter internship. That decision led me onto the path that would eventually become the backbone of my career: health policy and health information technology.

The military's efforts to develop an electronic health record to install in all military medical treatment facilities became an eye-opening learning ground for me. I was fascinated by the intersection of technology, healthcare delivery, and policy—how systems could be designed to improve care, how information could flow to support better decisions, how the right infrastructure could transform entire organizations.

After completing the internship, I moved back to New England to work as a management engineer in a large health system in Massachusetts, then to Shared Medical Systems, installing their clinical information system in hospitals in the Boston area and in Albuquerque, New Mexico.

Both were very detail-oriented jobs. And I eventually realized I wasn't suited to that type of work. The endless specifications, the technical minutiae, the focus on trees rather than forests—it drained me. I aspired to work that felt more meaningful, where I could have an impact at a broader level, where I could think strategically about systems rather than implementing tactical solutions.

Finding My Way

After moving back to Washington D.C., I took a position in the Office of the Assistant Secretary of Defense for Health Affairs as a policy analyst. This, I thought, would give me the opportunity to work at that broader level I craved.

I loved the experience, but I found the job a bit too bureaucratic—too many layers, too much process, too little actual impact. Restless and thinking I might have entrepreneurial leanings, I left for what I thought would be an opportunity with a small company working for the military. This was my entry into the world of government contracting, a whole ecosystem unto itself that makes employment inside and around the beltway in Washington, DC tick.

I was immediately thrust back into detail-oriented work—training on systems I didn't know much about—and I quickly became disillusioned. I also came face to face with my introverted self in a new way. The job required steady face-to-face interaction that drained my energy completely. By the end of each day, I felt hollowed out, exhausted in a way that had nothing to do with the work itself and everything to do with the constant external stimulation.

After a year, I moved back into government, into a somewhat more senior policy position. Finally, I began the journey I had originally set out to do: developing strategy and architecture for the military health system information technology infrastructure.

I was excited. I was energized. And I wanted to learn more about this nascent yet quickly developing field of health information technology.

The Doctoral Journey

So I did what I always did when I wanted to understand something deeply: I went back to school.

I embarked upon a five-year journey toward a doctorate in health policy and strategic management, with a focus on information technology. It was brutal, going to school part-time while working full-time. There were nights when I fell asleep over journal articles at my kitchen table. Weekends disappeared into literature reviews and data analysis. My social life became virtually nonexistent, though as an introvert, that bothered me less than it might have bothered others.

But the synergy between my work and my studies was a perfect fit. The big questions in my mind—How do hospitals use information technology to develop and implement their strategies? How do the strategic planning and IT planning processes align? Are organizations that are more strategically oriented more inclined to use information technology for strategic purposes? How do these things impact hospital performance?—these questions were driving both my research and my daily work.

My dissertation examined the relationship between strategic orientation, strategic resource orientation, and performance in acute care hospitals. It was exactly the kind of complex systems thinking that fascinated me—looking at patterns, connections, and emergent properties in organizational behavior.

The writing was exhausting. The defense was terrifying. But I successfully defended my lengthy dissertation and was awarded a Doctor of Philosophy.

How did I feel? Accomplished, certainly. Relieved, absolutely. And a bit uncertain about what might come next.

Looking back, I can see the pattern that was always there, even when I couldn't name it. From the girl who came home from elementary school with her arms full of books to the woman defending her doctoral dissertation, the through-line was constant: a deep, insatiable need to understand.

To understand the world, to understand systems, to understand how things work and why they work that way and how they might work better. This drive for knowledge and mastery was both a gift and a burden. It pushed me forward, propelled me through challenges, gave me purpose. But it also meant I could never quite rest, never quite feel that I knew enough, never quite shake the fear that I was still somehow inadequate despite all the degrees and accomplishments.

The black sheep was still trying to prove she belonged, even as she was carving out her own unique path. The middle child was still trying to be noticed, even as she was building expertise that would eventually make her impossible to ignore.

I had chosen healthcare because I wanted to help people, to do good, to change the world. I had found my particular niche at the intersection of policy, management, and technology—a place where I could think about complex systems and strategic possibilities, where I could work at a level that felt meaningful.

Yet, I was still searching for something I couldn't quite name. Some sense of being enough, of having arrived, of finally proving that I was as smart and capable as I had always needed to be.

The quest for understanding would continue. Soon, it would take me in directions I never anticipated—into leadership roles that would test everything I thought I knew about myself, into personal challenges that would require every bit of resilience I had developed, and ultimately into a kind of reinvention I couldn't yet imagine.

For now, though, I had my doctorate. I had my expertise. I had my career path.

What I didn't yet understand was that all this knowledge, all this intellectual mastery, would not be enough to prepare me for what was coming. The real lessons—about leadership, about resilience, about what it means to be human in an interconnected world—those would require a different kind of education entirely.

CHAPTER 3

Climbing the Ladder

I grew up in the midst of the feminist movement of the 1960s, 70s, and 80s. My mother and the women around me encouraged education, career, independence. The message was clear: you can be anything, do anything, achieve anything. Focus on your career. Build something of your own.

For the next decade of my life, I did just that.

Although I was socially active, my personal life, relationships, and any thought of family took a back seat to my career. A relationship I began in my early thirties lingered, off and on, for many years, existing in that uncomfortable space between commitment and convenience. It would eventually end rather abruptly in my early forties, setting me on a path I never would have expected.

But I'm getting ahead of myself.

Learning the Business

Shortly after completing my Ph.D., I left government to start a consulting practice within a small business working in the federal health and state health and social services markets. It was an opportunity to further spread my wings, to fuel my ongoing desire to grow and learn. I was excited to delve into the business world and learn the ins and outs of the professional services trade.

The next five years were a master class in the professional services business and in creating a consulting practice from the ground up.

I learned to develop new service offerings and marketing strategies. I learned to create business plans and growth strategies, building a consulting practice from virtually nothing. I learned the fundamentals of marketing and financial management in professional services. I learned about program and project planning and management—the difference between what you promise and what you can actually deliver, how to scope work realistically, how to manage client expectations while pushing for excellence.

I learned how to recruit, hire, and train new staff. I learned how to motivate and inspire people, to help them see possibilities they couldn't see in themselves. This was the beginning of my leadership journey, though I didn't recognize it as such at the time. I thought I was just learning how to run a business.

Learning the business side was valuable, and it would serve me well throughout my career. It wasn't where my heart was though. As I transitioned into more senior leadership roles, I began to understand that the financial aspects of the business drove everything, and that as a leader, this was where you were expected to lead from—the bottom line, the revenue projections, the margins.

It wasn't that I didn't understand business drivers and financials. I did. There were just other things that grabbed my attention, that lit me up: How do you know what products and services to sell? To whom? Where? Who are the competitors? Who are our target clients? How do we position ourselves in the market to compete? How do we market our services? What methods do we use to understand the market and where we fit?

Through my doctoral work, I had learned theories, methods, and practices from renowned experts on business and strategy. Now I was trying to weave these into actual business strategy, watching them come alive as I cut my teeth in the world of consulting. This was systems thinking in action, strategy as a living practice rather than an academic exercise.

From the opposite side of the fence from where I once sat as a federal client, I learned what it meant to deliver exceptional services—and the internal gyrations that companies go through to meet client needs. I learned how to scout and capture new business. I learned the incredibly complex process of federal acquisitions and the sometimes arcane rules that govern it. I learned how different the state health and human services market is from the federal marketplace, and the intricacies of how federal funding flows to state programs.

What continued to light my fire wasn't the business mechanics. It was the ability to have a real impact on the lives of people who depended on the services our clients delivered. This was the through-line from my earliest desire to "do good" and change the world. I might not be treating patients directly, but I could improve the systems that served them.

Hawaii: A Different Pace

I had the opportunity to live this firsthand when I supported a state Medicaid program in revamping its business processes, information systems, and technology infrastructure. The client was on the other side of the country and an ocean away from my home base, which meant living away from home for the better part of two years.

Personally, this was hard. The distance, the separation from everything familiar, the strain of maintaining a relationship that was already hanging on by a thread—in the end, it probably contributed to the slow death of that relationship.

But what Hawaii gave me was the opportunity to live in a different culture and experience life at a different pace than what I was used to after growing up and living on the East Coast for most of my life.

I learned to adapt to living and working in a culture where priorities were fundamentally different: family first, work second. That didn't mean work didn't get done. It meant leaving work at the end of the workday, not taking it home, being fully present during work hours and fully absent after. Coming off five years of the rigorous schedule of work and doctoral school, this took some adjustment. I'm not sure I ever entirely adapted, though I did learn to slow down and, occasionally, smell the roses.

The benefits were huge. I had time to travel, to immerse myself in native Hawaiian culture, to enjoy the beach, to indulge in the amazing food. I learned that there were different ways to live, different values that could organize a life. It was a lesson I would need later, though I didn't know it yet.

At the end of the consulting engagement, I headed home and settled into a more or less routine life. My passion for exercise and keeping myself healthy remained, and I took up competitive running and triathlons.

Training consumed an enormous amount of time. As much as I enjoyed it, I sometimes wondered if it was really an escape for me—from something. Eventually, I realized what I loved was the training itself, pushing myself to my personal best, the discipline and structure of following a plan. Competition, on the other hand, was stressful. I often overtrained, leading to regular injuries.

Eventually, I would give up the competition and just enjoy running, swimming, and cycling. They had become my way to decompress and manage the depressive tendencies that sometimes reared their head—the darkness that would creep in when I slowed down long enough to feel it.

The Pattern Emerges

After a few years, I began to get restless. I started to look for a new opportunity.

This would become a pattern: two to three years to master a new job, then move on to the next. Lack of opportunity for growth often pushed me to look elsewhere, as did opportunities that would expand my knowledge and experience and allow me to have an impact in a new, sometimes bigger arena.

Some opportunities panned out. Some did not.

Some led me down roads that looked great on paper and seemed like a good fit. In spite of the due diligence I thought I had done, once I was onboard and living the culture of the organization, it became clear the fit wasn't right or it wasn't what I was looking for. And there were opportunities I didn't fully vet as carefully as I should have—those rarely worked out.

In time, I recognized that some moves were not really about the opportunity itself. I was looking for an escape from something that had become uncomfortable, untenable, or no longer supportive of my quest to always be learning and growing. I was running again, but this time from jobs instead of on roads, from routine and the minutia of work that felt like distraction from the real work to be done.

I was pretty quick to realize when I had made a mistake and the situation wasn't as I had believed it to be. I always tried to give things a chance, to extend the benefit of the doubt. When it became clear a path wasn't right for me, I reassessed and often moved on.

Some viewed this as giving up. To me, it was my way of continuing to grow and learn. Looking back, I can see it was also about something else: the fear that if I stayed too long, my insecurities would start to emerge. Better to leave before I had the chance to fail.

Over time, I came to believe that what really matters—what can make or break the success of a leader—is alignment on strategy and values.

Do your personal values align with those of the organization, and especially those of the leaders? This often requires a deep dive on the organization, which can be hard to do from the outside. Be clear on what you're looking for and particularly what the make-or-break conditions are. What matters to you most in your day-to-day life? How do your values line up with the mission, vision, and espoused values of the organization? What do you know about what's actually practiced—do the espoused values align with the lived values and practices? What are you willing to live with if they don't align? How will you know?

I didn't fully appreciate the role that values played in my life and my choices until much later, during a pivotal period in my career. The seeds of that understanding were being planted during these years of job-hopping and searching.

When it became clear that I was not aligned on strategy with the CEO of a company I had just joined, I left after six months. I hung my shingle as an independent consultant and for the next three years consulted with federal agencies on impactful work for beneficiaries of federal health and benefits programs.

My work spanned strategic management, business process redesign, health IT strategy, data analytics, program management, and policy development at the forefront of health policy and practice at the federal level. I loved the work, and I loved the independence of working for myself on such meaningful projects. My clients were among the hardest working and most committed people I knew.

Through this work and the deep dive on health IT strategy in my doctoral research, I saw the possibilities in health information technology as a strategic enabler in healthcare on a much broader scale than what was currently in practice. This felt like the path forward—the place where I could have the biggest impact, where systems thinking and strategic management and technology all converged.

I was building something. I was growing. I was making a difference.

And then everything fell apart.

The Year Everything Changed

The following year, my life was torn apart and turned upside down.

Within the span of twelve months, I started a new job, ended a long-term relationship, and lost my dad. In the middle of this, terrorists attacked the United States.

By the end of the year, I knew I would never be the same again.

The year 2001 was a turning point for me. I started it in a new job, one I thought would be an opportunity to take a leadership role in the health IT business of a major corporation. I was enticed out of my consulting work, back into the corporate world, giving up a lucrative consulting practice that, for all its benefits and all that it offered, left me unfulfilled as a leader.

I was driven to see what I could accomplish as a leader building a business under the umbrella of a corporate enterprise. What seemed like a great opportunity—leading the healthcare practice in a large IT company—would be short-lived.

The day before I was to start, I learned that the job I had accepted was going to change. The parent company had just acquired five companies, three of which had health lines of business. These were targeted to be combined into one integrated business unit.

When I learned I was likely not in line to lead the new unit, it threw me into a tailspin. Having given up my consulting practice and cancelled contracts with valued clients in the process, I was angry and anxious about the uncertainty of my future. The ground had shifted beneath me before I'd even started.

Eventually, I landed in a role that seemed well suited to me: leading the integration of the health business units and developing strategy for the new business unit. It still felt like a slap in the face and perhaps tugged at my deep-seated feelings of inadequacy. But it did tap into my strategic abilities, my insights into the market, and my interest in strategic management.

It meant collaborating across fractured companies whose leaders were jockeying for position and promotion. It challenged my skills in interpersonal relations and negotiation. I came to view it as a growth opportunity—leading the development of business strategy for a two-hundred-million-dollar business unit in a large corporation.

It also tested my will and determination in pushing gender boundaries.

The Glass Ceiling

Being a female in a male-dominant corporate culture, I came head-to-head with a very thick glass ceiling I had not encountered before. I wasn't fully prepared for the battles I had to fight and was somewhat taken aback by the prevailing view of women in leadership.

I did not fit the masculine mold of a leader. My collaborative and participative style of leadership was an anathema in the autocratic and transactional corporate culture. While I was trying to build consensus and bring people along, the men around me were issuing directives and expecting compliance. While I was asking questions and seeking input, they were making declarations and moving on.

I was told, more than once, that I was "too nice" to be a leader. That I needed to be "tougher," more "commanding." The implicit message was clear: to succeed here, you need to be more like a man.

I pushed back in my own way, quietly insisting on my approach, trying to demonstrate that there was another way to lead. It was exhausting, constantly swimming against the current, constantly having to justify my style, constantly feeling like I had to work twice as hard to be seen as half as competent. That being said, all the people and teams I led consistently expressed how much they appreciated my leadership style.

The black sheep was butting up against another flock that didn't want her.

Crises Converge

And then, in February of that year, my dad was diagnosed with advanced-stage lung cancer.

I was hopeful yet cautious as he entered radiation therapy and chemotherapy. It took a huge toll on him—the man who had been such a strong swimmer, who had spearfished in the waters off Block Island, who had designed computer systems and built his own house, was suddenly frail and diminished.

As I navigated the stressful work environment and his declining health, I was confronted with yet another personal crisis. My long-term relationship was failing. In the early days of summer, it finally, definitively ended.

I floundered personally as every aspect of my life was affected. I tried to hold it together and managed to do so reasonably well—keeping up appearances at work, being there for my parents, maintaining the routines that kept me functional.

Until the unthinkable happened.

On September 11th, the United States was attacked by terrorists.

I remember vividly watching the planes crash into the World Trade Center and the Pentagon on the news. It was all surreal—the images repeating on every channel, the smoke billowing, the towers collapsing, the footage of people running through streets thick with ash. I remember trying to get home in the crush of people streaming out of downtown Washington, DC. The fear and panic were palpable. Hours later, I arrived home, numb to what had transpired and what it meant for our country and our lives.

Living within a few miles of the Pentagon, the event lingered for weeks on end as smoke wafted across the area. Every day, driving past, seeing the damage, smelling the acrid air—it was a constant reminder that the world had fundamentally changed.

Already on edge and emotionally stretched to the limit, I was barely holding on when, a week later, the cancer flooding my dad's body metastasized to his brain.

The news hit me like a ton of bricks. There was no coming back from this. No more hoping, no more fighting, no more treatment plans. Just the terrible, inevitable progression toward the end.

I hit a wall.

I was emotionally numb, unable to feel anything beyond a distant, hollow ache. As I always did, I kept it all inside and tried to navigate terrain that kept shifting beneath my feet. I went to work. I visited my father. I went through the motions. I held my mother's hand while my own heart was breaking.

Less than three months later, he passed away.

I tried to be there for my mom, dealing with my own grief over the loss of a parent, a failed long-term relationship, and a career that felt off the rails. I had lost my footing in every part of my life. Everything that had felt solid—work, relationship, family structure, even the safety of the country itself—had been revealed as fragile, temporary, subject to forces beyond my control.

By the end of the year, I knew something had to change.

I couldn't keep climbing this ladder. I couldn't keep pushing harder, achieving more, proving myself over and over in systems that didn't value what I had to offer. I couldn't keep running—from jobs, from feelings, from the deep sense that despite all my accomplishments, I still wasn't enough.

The Lessons Taking Shape

The lessons from this period would take years to fully understand. At the time, I was simply surviving, getting through each day, trying not to think too hard about what any of it meant.

But looking back, I can see what was emerging:

The importance of values alignment—not just knowing your values intellectually, but living them, and being willing to walk away from opportunities that violate them.

The reality of gender barriers in leadership, and the cost of constantly having to prove yourself in systems designed for someone else.

The danger of using achievement as a way to avoid feeling, using constant motion to outrun the darkness.

The fragility of everything we take for granted —health, relationships, safety, life itself.

And perhaps most importantly: the limits of the model I had been following. The feminist promise that I could have it all, do it all, be it all—career success, relationship, health, impact—was revealing itself as incomplete. Something was missing. Something was unsustainable about the pace I was keeping, the expectations I was trying to meet, the person I was trying to be.

The ladder I had been climbing was leaning against the wrong wall. I just didn't know yet what the right wall looked like, or if I even wanted to keep climbing at all. The black sheep had proven she could succeed in the corporate world. She had the doctorate, the consulting practice, the strategic leadership role, the business acumen. She had climbed the ladder, pushed through barriers, and survived multiple crises.

But she was exhausted. And she was starting to wonder if all this proving had been in service of the wrong question.

The quest for understanding was about to take an unexpected turn—away from external achievement and toward something much harder to master: understanding what it meant to build a life, not just a career. Understanding what was truly worth fighting for.

But first, there would be more climbing. More opportunities, more challenges, more lessons learned the hard way. The breaking point was still years away. But the cracks were beginning to show.

CHAPTER 4

The Unexpected Path

The years following my father's death were a study in rebuilding. I had survived 2001—barely—and now I had to figure out what came next. The corporate world had proven itself both fascinating and hostile, a place where I could demonstrate strategic thinking but never quite belong. The ladder I had been climbing felt increasingly unstable, yet I couldn't seem to stop reaching for the next rung.

What I didn't yet understand was that the most profound lessons weren't waiting at the top of any ladder. They were waiting in the spaces between certainty and chaos, in the moments when carefully laid plans collided with messy reality, in the recognition that leadership isn't about control but about navigating complexity with grace and intention.

This chapter of my career would teach me that.

A New Beginning, Again

After leaving the corporate environment where I had butted up against that thick glass ceiling, I returned to consulting. But this time, I wasn't alone. I joined forces with a partner to build a small consulting firm focused on health IT strategy and implementation.

It felt like coming home to myself in some ways —back to the work I loved, the strategic thinking that energized me, the mission-driven projects that gave meaning to the long hours. We worked with federal agencies and healthcare organizations, helping them navigate the rapidly evolving landscape of health information technology.

This was the mid-2000s, and healthcare IT was transforming from a niche technical concern into a national priority. Electronic health records were moving from the margins to the mainstream. The promise of technology to improve patient safety, reduce costs, and transform care delivery was capturing attention at the highest levels of government and industry.

I was in my element. The work required exactly the kind of systems thinking I had spent years developing—seeing how pieces fit together, understanding how changes in one part of a system ripple through the whole, anticipating unintended consequences, planning for emergence rather than trying to control every variable.

Building a consulting firm also meant learning new lessons about leadership, about partnership, about the gap between vision and execution.

Working with a partner brought both tremendous energy and significant friction. We complemented each other in many ways—different strengths, different networks, different approaches to problems. This diversity could be powerful when we were aligned.

Alignment proved harder to maintain than I had anticipated.

We had different working styles. I was the INTJ strategist—wanting to think deeply, plan thoroughly, consider all angles before acting. My partner was more action-oriented, preferring to move quickly and adjust course as needed. Neither approach was wrong, but they didn't always mesh smoothly.

We had different values around work-life balance, around what success looked like, around how to treat employees and clients. These differences, minor at first, grew more pronounced as the business grew. What had seemed like complementary perspectives began to feel like fundamental incompatibilities.

I found myself once again in the role of mediator, trying to bridge differences, find middle ground, keep the peace. The middle child was back at work, doing what she had always done—managing tensions, seeing both sides, trying to make everyone happy.

Except I was exhausted by it. And I was starting to recognize a pattern in my own behavior: I kept putting myself in situations where I had to prove I could make things work, where I had to demonstrate my value by solving impossible problems, where my worth was measured by my ability to handle what others couldn't.

The seeds of overcommitment were taking root, though I didn't recognize them as such. I thought I was just being dedicated. Thorough. Excellent.

Systems Thinking in Action

Despite the partnership challenges, the work itself was deeply satisfying. I was getting to apply everything I had learned—from my doctoral research, from my years in policy development, from my time in both government and private sector—to real-world problems with significant impact.

One project stands out vividly in my memory. We were working with a large federal health agency to develop a comprehensive IT strategy that would support their mission over the next decade. It required understanding not just technology, but policy, operations, workforce capabilities, budget constraints, political dynamics, and organizational culture.

This was the kind of complex adaptive system that fascinated me. Nothing happened in isolation. Every decision created ripples. Every change in one area affected multiple other areas in ways that weren't always predictable. You couldn't just draw a straight line from the current state to the desired future state and march along it. You had to build in flexibility, create space for emergence, plan for learning and adjustment.

I remember sitting in a conference room with stakeholders from across the agency—clinicians, IT staff, policy experts, administrators, finance people—all with different priorities, different mental models, different languages for talking about the same challenges. My job was to help them see the connections, understand the interdependencies, and build a shared vision of what was possible.

It was like conducting an orchestra where every musician was playing from a different score. The challenge wasn't just technical or strategic—it was deeply human. It required listening to what people weren't saying, sensing the undercurrents of resistance and hope, finding language that could bridge silos.

This was leadership, I realized. Not the command-and-control leadership I had rejected in the corporate world, but something more nuanced and powerful: the ability to hold complexity, to help groups navigate uncertainty, to create conditions for collective intelligence to emerge.

I was good at this. Really good. And for perhaps the first time in my career, I felt like I was doing work that fully utilized who I was—my strategic mind, my empathic abilities, my systems thinking, my need to make a difference.

But success brought its own dangers.

As our reputation grew, so did the demands on my time. Clients wanted me specifically on their projects. Partners wanted my strategic input on proposals. Staff wanted mentoring and guidance. My business partner needed me to balance their more impulsive tendencies with careful analysis.

I said yes to almost everything. I told myself I was building the business, serving clients well, being a good partner and mentor. I told myself this was what leadership required—showing up, being available, going the extra mile.

What I didn't see was the trap I was building for myself.

I was becoming indispensable, which felt like success but was actually a symptom of dysfunction. A healthy system doesn't require any one person to be everywhere, doing everything. But I was creating exactly that situation—through my own need to be needed, to prove my worth, to justify my place in the world.

The black sheep was still trying to prove she belonged, still trying to demonstrate she was good enough. And the way I knew to do that was through work, through achievement, through being the one who could handle anything.

I worked long hours. I took calls in the evenings and on weekends. I traveled constantly—DC to San Francisco, DC to Boston, DC to Atlanta, sometimes multiple cities in a single week. I reviewed every major deliverable personally, not trusting others to maintain the quality standards I demanded.

My standards were high. Too high, probably. Perfectionism masked as excellence, driven by the fear that any mistake would reveal me as the fraud I sometimes still felt like, despite all evidence to the contrary.

I maintained my exercise routine—running in hotel fitness centers, swimming in whatever pool was available, cycling on weekends when I was home. Exercise was still my primary stress management tool, my way of clearing my head, my portal to something like peace.

But I was running on fumes. I just didn't know it yet.

Pushing Boundaries

One of my strengths as a leader was my willingness to push boundaries—to question conventional wisdom, to propose unconventional approaches, to challenge the "we've always done it this way" mentality that stifles innovation.

This served my clients well. I helped organizations think bigger, see possibilities they hadn't considered, imagine futures they thought were impossible. I was good at asking the questions no one else was asking, at spotting patterns others missed, at connecting dots that seemed unrelated.

Boundary-pushing has a shadow side. Sometimes I push too hard, too fast. Sometimes my impatience with incremental change led me to propose solutions that organizations weren't ready to implement. Sometimes my confidence in my strategic vision blinded me to legitimate concerns about feasibility, resources, or timing.

And sometimes—though I didn't fully recognize this until much later—I was pushing boundaries not because it was what the situation required, but because being the provocateur, the challenger, the rebel was how I maintained my identity as the black sheep. Being different, being unconventional, not accepting the status quo—this was who I had always been. It was my brand, my value proposition, my way of standing out.

It was also exhausting. And it made collaboration harder than it needed to be.

I remember one project where I proposed a radical restructuring of how a healthcare organization approached its IT governance. The proposal was sound—it addressed real problems, it would create better alignment between IT investments and strategic priorities, it would improve decision-making.

I had moved too fast. I hadn't built enough support before proposing the change. I hadn't sufficiently addressed the political dynamics that would make implementation difficult. I had been so focused on the technical and strategic aspects that I had underestimated the human factors.

The proposal was ultimately rejected. Not because it was wrong, but because I hadn't created the conditions for it to be adopted. I had pushed the boundary without building the bridge. It was a humbling lesson, one I would need to learn multiple times before it truly sank in: being right isn't enough. Being strategic isn't enough. You also have to be wise about timing, about relationships, about the pace of change people can actually absorb.

My doctoral work had taught me about strategic planning—the importance of analysis, of setting clear goals, of developing roadmaps and action plans. My INTJ personality reinforced this preference for structure, for thinking things through thoroughly before acting.

My real-world experience was teaching me something else: that no plan survives contact with reality unchanged. That the most important skill isn't creating the perfect plan, but being able to adapt when the plan encounters the messiness of actual implementation.

This tension—between planning and emergence, between control and flexibility, between structure and flow—became a central theme of my leadership development during these years.

I watched organizations spend months developing comprehensive strategic plans that were outdated before the ink dried. I saw IT implementation projects derailed not by technical problems but by organizational dynamics no one had anticipated. I experienced the frustration of watching carefully crafted strategies fail because they couldn't adapt quickly enough to changing circumstances.

And I began to understand that effective leadership required holding both sides of this paradox: the need for structure and the necessity of flexibility, the value of planning and the importance of responding to what emerges, the discipline of staying focused on goals and the wisdom of knowing when to adjust them.

This wasn't either/or. It was both/and.

The best strategies, I learned, were those that provided clear direction while remaining open to adjustment. The best leaders were those who could plan meticulously while staying alert to what was actually happening, who could hold firmly to purpose while remaining flexible about approach.

I was learning to do this, slowly and imperfectly. To plan thoroughly and hold plans lightly. To be decisive and remain curious. To have strong opinions loosely held.

I was also learning that this kind of adaptive leadership was cognitively and emotionally demanding. It required being comfortable with ambiguity, with not knowing, with changing course when new information emerged. It required the confidence to commit to a direction and the humility to reverse course when needed.

For someone whose sense of safety came from understanding, from mastery, from having everything figured out, this was challenging territory. The black sheep who had spent her life trying to prove she was smart enough, competent enough, good enough—she didn't want to admit uncertainty. She didn't want to change plans because that felt like admitting the original plan was wrong.

And leadership was demanding exactly that: the ability to hold complexity, to embrace uncertainty, to be confident and humble simultaneously.

I was growing into this capacity. But the growth was painful, and I was paying for it with my own energy, my own resources, my own well-being.

The Warning Signs

Looking back, I can see the warning signs that I missed at the time. Or perhaps I saw them and chose to ignore them, telling myself I was fine, I could handle it, I just needed to push through a little longer.

I was tired all the time. Not just physically tired from travel and long hours, but a deeper exhaustion that didn't resolve with a good night's sleep or a weekend off. I was running on adrenaline and willpower, sustained by coffee and the satisfaction of completing projects, checking things off lists, solving problems.

My eating habits had deteriorated. I ate on the run, grabbed whatever was convenient, skipped meals when I was too busy to stop. Then compensated by overeating when I finally slowed down.

My relationships were suffering. I was so focused on work that I had little energy left for friends, for dating, for the kind of social connection that sustains people through difficult times. I told myself I was just in a busy season, that things would ease up soon, that I could catch up on relationships later.

Later never came. There was always another project, another deadline, another crisis that needed my attention. My body was sending me messages I didn't want to hear. Frequent headaches. Trouble sleeping despite being exhausted. A persistent sense of being wound too tight, like a spring compressed to its limit.

I kept going. Because that's what I did. I was the one who could handle anything, who never gave up, who always delivered. The black sheep proved she was strong, capable, worthy of her place in the world. Despite the toll it was taking, these years represented significant leadership maturity for me. I was developing capacities I hadn't possessed earlier in my career:

– The ability to see multiple perspectives simultaneously and help groups find common ground.

- The skill of translating between different organizational languages—technical and clinical, strategic and operational, executive and frontline.
- The wisdom to know when to push and when to wait, when to challenge and when to support, when to lead from the front and when to lead from behind.
- The confidence to bring my whole self to my work—my strategic mind, my empathic abilities, my systems thinking, my quirky perspective that saw things others missed.

I was becoming the leader I had always wanted to be: someone who could hold complexity, navigate uncertainty, create conditions for collective intelligence to emerge, help systems evolve toward greater health and effectiveness.

I was also becoming someone else: someone who didn't know how to stop, who measured her worth by her achievements, who had lost the ability to rest, to play, to simply be rather than constantly do.

The feminist promise that I could have it all was revealing its dark side. I could have career success—but at the cost of relationships, health, balance. I could be a respected leader—but only by giving everything to the work and leaving nothing for myself.

I didn't see the trap I was in. Or perhaps I did see it but couldn't imagine a way out. This was who I was: the high achiever, the strategic thinker, the problem solver, the woman who could handle anything.

Stopping wasn't an option. Slowing down wasn't possible. Admitting I was struggling would mean admitting I wasn't as strong as I needed to be.

So I kept going.

Seeds of What Was Coming

The seeds of overcommitment that would eventually lead to burnout were planted during these years, though I didn't recognize them as such. I thought I was building a career, developing expertise, and making an impact. I thought I was finally becoming the leader I had always aspired to be.

And I was. But I was also building a house of cards, held together by willpower and adrenaline, sustained by my need to prove myself rather than grounded in sustainable practices.

The pattern was clear to anyone who was looking: work harder, achieve more, move on to the next challenge without pausing to integrate the lessons, without rest, without reflection, without replenishment. Keep climbing, keep proving, keep running—from what, I didn't know. Toward what, I couldn't say.

I was mastering the art of leadership as a practice, as a set of skills and capacities. But I hadn't learned the most important lesson: that sustainable leadership requires taking care of the leader. That you can't pour from an empty cup. That burning yourself out in service of the mission doesn't serve anyone in the long run.

These lessons were coming.

First, I would need to hit bottom.

First, I would need to experience what happens when the overcommitment and perfectionism and need to prove yourself collide with the inevitable limits of human capacity.

First, I would need to break. Completely. Undeniably. In ways that couldn't be fixed by working harder or being smarter or pushing through one more time. That was still ahead. For now, I was at the height of my professional powers, doing work I found meaningful, respected by clients and colleagues, building expertise in a field that mattered.

I was successful by every external measure. And I was slowly, quietly, coming apart at the seams.

This period of my career taught me something crucial about leadership: that the path forward isn't always the obvious one. That growth often comes from unexpected directions. That the most important lessons are frequently the ones we don't plan for.

I had spent years climbing ladders, pursuing goals, striving for achievement. And I had accomplished a great deal. But the path that would transform me most profoundly wasn't the one I was on. It was waiting around a corner I hadn't yet turned, in a direction I hadn't thought to look.

The unexpected path wasn't about career advancement or professional achievement. It was about something far more fundamental: learning what it means to be human, to be vulnerable, to need help, to be enough without proving anything.

I couldn't learn those lessons through work alone. I couldn't strategize my way to that understanding. I couldn't think my way through it or plan my way around it.

I would have to live it. And living it would require a kind of courage I didn't yet know I possessed. The black sheep was about to step off the path entirely, into territory she had never imagined. Into a transformation she hadn't planned for, didn't expect, and couldn't control.

Into motherhood.

Before that unexpected gift, before that transformative leap of faith, I would continue on this path a while longer—gathering tools I didn't know I was collecting, learning lessons I didn't realize I was learning, building capacities I would desperately need for what was coming.

The quest for understanding was about to become intensely personal. The systems thinking I had applied to organizations was about to be tested on the most complex adaptive system of all: a family I would create through adoption, against all conventional wisdom, in the middle of an already demanding career. The boundary-pushing would take on new meaning. The balance between planning and emergence would be tested in ways I couldn't imagine. The seeds of overcommitment would grow into a full-blown crisis that would force a reckoning with everything I thought I knew about strength and success.

But that's getting ahead of the story. For now, I was still the successful consultant, the strategic thinker, the problem solver, the woman who had proven she could make it in a man's world, who had built a career on her own terms, who had survived loss and disappointment and kept moving forward.

I thought I knew who I was. I thought I understood what mattered. I thought I had learned the most important lessons leadership had to teach. I was wrong about all of it. The unexpected path was waiting. And it would change everything.

CHAPTER 5

A Solo Leap of Faith

The year after my father's death, I made the most improbable decision of my life.

I decided to adopt a child. Alone. In my early forties, with a demanding career, no partner, and no experience with children beyond playing aunt to my sister's and brother's kids.

When I tell people this now, they often say it sounds brave. At the time, it felt less like bravery and more like responding to something I could no longer ignore—a pull so strong that all my careful planning, all my strategic thinking, all my need to have everything figured out simply couldn't override it.

This was not the plan. This was never the plan.

Sometimes the most important decisions we make aren't the ones we plan for. They're the ones that choose us, that insist themselves into our carefully constructed lives, that demand we become someone we didn't know we could be.

The Awakening

I had never thought much about having children. Growing up in the feminist movement of the 1960s,

70s, and 80s, surrounded by messages about education, career, and independence, I absorbed a clear directive: build something of your own. Focus on your career. You can be anything, do anything, achieve anything.

And I did. I built a career I was proud of. I earned my doctorate. I became a respected consultant and strategist. I proved I could make it in spaces that weren't designed for women like me.

When the thought of children did occasionally surface, I convinced myself it wasn't something I wanted. I was independent. I liked my freedom. I traveled for work, worked long hours, pursued athletic challenges that consumed my weekends. Where would a child fit into this life I had so carefully constructed?

Besides, I told myself, not everyone needs to have children. Not everyone should.

But then my sister Caryn and brother Brian had children.

I started spending time with my niece and nephews, and something shifted. I watched my father with his grandchildren—his unbounded joy, the softness that emerged when he held them, the way he would get down on the floor to play despite his age. I saw a dimension of love I hadn't fully appreciated before.

I felt something stirring that I couldn't name. A sense that perhaps there was something missing in my life that I hadn't allowed myself to acknowledge.

By my late thirties, the thought became more insistent. A whisper that grew louder. A possibility that wouldn't let go. I knew the biological clock was ticking. If I was going to have a child, I needed to either get busy quickly or find a different way. But I was single, with no relationship on the horizon. The long-term relationship I had maintained, off and on, for nearly a decade had finally, definitively ended. I was alone, approaching an age where pregnancy would be increasingly difficult, if not impossible.

I began to think about adoption. Just think about it. Letting the idea percolate without committing to anything.

At first, I rejected it outright. What made me think I could possibly handle the stress of parenting solo? Would I be a good parent? Could I be a good parent? How would I pursue my career while being a mother? The questions circled endlessly, each one a reason to dismiss the whole idea.

But the thought stuck. It wafted in and out of my consciousness with increasing regularity. When a close friend mentioned that his cousin adopted as a single mother, I began to take the possibility more seriously.

Still, I did nothing. I was good at strategic planning, at analyzing options, at thinking things through. But this decision felt too big, too permanent, too life-altering to approach rationally.

The Catalyst

When my father died in the fall of 2001, something crystallized.

In the midst of my grief, watching my mother's devastation, remembering my father's joy with his grandchildren, I understood with sudden clarity: I wanted this. I needed this. And I was running out of time. My dad loved his grandchildren with a fierce, uncomplicated love. It made me profoundly sad that I would never be able to share that with him, that he would never know my child. His death convinced me that I needed to break free of the fear I had been holding inside.

Fear of not being good enough. Fear of failing. Fear of being too different, too independent, too focused on my career to be a good mother. Fear that wanting this meant admitting I couldn't have it all on my own terms after all.

The black sheep who had spent her life proving she could chart her own course was about to take the most unconventional path yet.

My mother was the first person I told. "I'm thinking about adopting a child," I said, half expecting resistance, half hoping for it so I could use it as a reason to abandon the idea.

Her response stopped me cold: "I thought you should have done it a long time ago."

Knowing I had her support—her approval—gave me permission to move forward. To take seriously what had been just a possibility.

As I always did when embarking on something new, I immersed myself completely. I researched everything I could about adoption. I learned that as a single woman, international adoption was my best option. Russia had an active international adoption program and allowed single women to adopt. Given my Russian heritage through my mother's family, it felt like a meaningful connection.

I found an adoption agency nearby with an established program in Russia and began the process. Working with the adoption agency was simultaneously informative and overwhelming. They had experience, a team of facilitators and translators on the ground in Russia, established relationships with orphanages. But they also had to prepare prospective parents for realities that were difficult to hear.

There were classes on parenting, on adoption, on the benefits and risks of adopting a child from an orphanage where medical information was often minimal or nonexistent. There were exercises designed to help us understand what we were looking for, what we expected, what we feared.

In one of these exercises, I drew a sailboat—a memory of my childhood, of my father emerging from the ocean with his catch, of summer days on Block Island. Something I hoped to pass on to my own child. The image surprised me with its emotional weight. This wasn't just about having a child. It was about connection, legacy, passing forward the love I had received.

The more I learned, the more certain I became that this was the path I needed to be on, despite the challenges and uncertainties. The statistics about children adopted from institutions. The potential for developmental delays, attachment issues, medical problems. The ethical complexities of international adoption. The sheer expense—tens of thousands of dollars in fees, travel costs, and endless paperwork.

Certainty isn't always the same as comfort though. I was terrified.

Once I made the commitment, there was paperwork. Mountains of paperwork. Documents about my background, my family, my health, my mental health, my finances, my suitability to become a parent. Home studies where a social worker evaluated my home and my readiness. FBI background checks. Immigration forms. Russian translation of every document.

I expressed interest in adopting either a boy or a girl and was told I would likely be matched with a boy since most prospective parents wanted girls. The agency worked in two regions of Russia—Perm and Kamensk-Uralsky, cities near the Ural Mountains on the edge of Siberia. How children were matched with adoptive parents was murky. I wouldn't know anything about the baby I was matched with until much later in the process.

The waiting began. And the waiting, as everyone told me, was the hardest part.

The Interlude

Knowing that once I became a parent I would have little time to travel, and needing time to decompress from the brutal year I'd just survived, I did something that probably seemed crazy to everyone else: I booked a three-week hiking trip to Patagonia.

It was my way of processing. Of letting go. Of preparing myself for the transformation that was coming. I needed to release the pain of losing my father. The grief over the end of my long-term relationship. The trauma that 9/11 had left on all of us. I needed to be in nature, in my body, away from the strategic thinking and problem-solving that dominated my work life.

I spent three glorious weeks exploring Argentina and Chile. Hiking the Paine del Torre and Mount Fitz Roy. Experiencing Grey Glacier and Los Glaciares National Park. Immersing myself in the cultures of Santiago, Punta Arenas, El Calafate, and Buenos Aires. The physical challenge of the hikes. The vastness of the landscapes. The rhythm of walking day after day.

I finished the trip with a lifelong friend, Candace, and our endearing guide Andrés. By the end, I felt renewed. Ready. As ready as I would ever be.

When I returned home, my attention turned fully to the journey ahead. I prepared the house. Set up a baby's room. I attended more parenting classes. My friends threw me a baby shower—a gathering of colleagues and friends from different walks of my life, all celebrating this unconventional path I was taking.

And I waited. For the call that would change everything. It came only a few weeks after I returned from Patagonia.

"We have a child," the adoption coordinator said. "You need to be ready to go in a week."

Emotion overwhelmed me. Joy. Terror. Excitement. Panic. Everything at once.

Flights to book. Clothes to pack. Gifts to purchase for the orphanage staff. And cash.

Thousands of dollars in cash that I would need to carry through airports across Europe and into Russia, where all adoption transactions were paid in currency. The prospect terrified me.

I would be traveling with another couple from a neighboring town who were also adopting. We would become close friends through this journey.

The trip was long. Dulles to Frankfurt. Frankfurt to Moscow. Then a boisterous, rowdy flight from Moscow to Yekaterinburg on a small regional Russian airline. Our facilitator and translator met us and ferried us to our hotel. The next day, we went to the Department of Education to learn about the children we had been matched with. All I knew was that I was matched with a ten-month-old boy. When I heard his name—Andrey—my heart melted.

I was nervous. Scared. Not sure what the next day would bring.

The two-hour drive from Yekaterinburg to Kamensk-Uralsky took us through rural Russian countryside—fields of crops, small towns with rundown houses, babushkas selling food and wares on the roadside. Exactly as one imagines Russia to be. I would travel this road many times over the coming weeks. I can still see it in my dreams.

The Meeting

The orphanage—they called it a "baby house"—was not much to look at. It appeared quite run down from the outside. The playground was poorly maintained and looked sad. We were met by the Director, Dr. Tatiana, who gave us a tour and settled us into a playroom where we would meet our children.

My stomach was in knots. And then Luna, one of the caregivers, brought Andrey into the room.

He was tiny, with a mop of curly blond hair, an endearing smile, and bright blue eyes. The connection was immediate and overwhelming. This was my son. I knew it in my bones, in my heart, in some deep place that had nothing to do with rational decision-making.

But there was also the medical exam. The meeting with Dr. Tatiana to learn about Andrey's history. And what I learned gave me pause. His birthmother was fifteen years old, from a large family in Kamensk-Uralsky. A teenage romance. The birth father was unknown. Andrey's birth had been difficult—breech, complicated. He experienced seizures within hours of being born and spent days in the hospital with no certainty he would survive.

There were many medical issues. Probable alcohol exposure in the womb. Possible developmental delays. Unknown long-term impacts from the difficult birth and early seizures. I spent the afternoon with him—holding him, feeding him, playing with toys we had brought. Every moment was precious. Every moment was also terrifying because I knew what was coming.

Leaving the orphanage that day was heartbreaking. The older children playing outside surrounded our van, running after us as we pulled away. I wanted to take every one of them home.

That night, I had to make the most difficult decision of my life.

The Choice

Was I going to adopt Andrey?

I tried to weigh it rationally. His medical history against what I had felt holding him. The potential challenges ahead against the connection I had experienced. The risks against the possibility.

If I said no, I would have to go back to the beginning. Wait for another match. Start over. And Andrey would go through another failed match, another prospective parent who decided he was too risky, too complicated, too uncertain.

If I said yes, I would be committing to a path I couldn't fully see or understand. A child with significant unknowns. Potential special needs. Developmental delays. All of it while parenting solo, maintaining a demanding career, building a life for both of us.

I lay awake most of the night, running through scenarios, trying to think strategically about something that wasn't a strategic decision.

In the end, the decision was already made. In my heart, he was already my son. The moment Luna had carried him into that playroom, the moment he looked at me with those bright blue eyes, the moment I held him—the decision was made.

The next day, I signed the papers. My heart was full of joy that this little boy, abandoned by others, would be mine. That I would be his. That we would figure out the rest together.

More paperwork consumed the next few days. Documents requesting that this boy become my son. Forms and signatures and translations. And then it was back to the U.S. to wait again.

The next few months were agonizing. The adoption paperwork worked its way through the maze of the Russian system, much of which I didn't fully understand. I only knew that I was under review, being evaluated by people who held my future—and Andrey's future—in their hands. Would they decide I was suitable to be his parent?

I spent the time preparing for the court hearing. Rehearsing answers to questions I thought they might ask. Translating documents. Organizing files. Trying to control the uncontrollable through meticulous preparation.

Finally, in late June, I was notified that the adoption could move forward, pending court approval. A court date was scheduled for July 2nd in Kamensk-Uralsky.

Another scramble for flights, hotels, arrangements. Another long journey to Russia. The court hearing would be the first step—an important one. But even after approval, there would be a ten-day waiting period for any family members to object to the adoption. Ten more days of uncertainty, of holding my breath, of not quite believing this was really happening.

The hearing took place as scheduled. It was surreal—conducted entirely in Russian, with our translator, also named Tatiana, navigating the proceedings. I had prepared thoroughly, and the preparation paid off.

The adoption was approved.

I only learned later that the hearing almost didn't happen because Andrey's birth certificate wasn't signed. It took a Herculean effort by the adoption team to get it signed before the court hearing. Another reminder of how tenuous everything was, how many things could have gone wrong.

Elated, we spent July 4th in Yekaterinburg. Local Russians, recognizing us as American, wished us happy Independence Day as we wandered the streets. The irony wasn't lost on me—celebrating independence in Russia as I prepared to bind my life to a child I had known for mere hours.

The next three weeks were wonderful and terrible in equal measure. We visited the baby house every other day, spending as much time as possible with Andrey. On alternate days, I walked endlessly around Yekaterinburg, learning the culture, killing time, waiting.

The adoption papers were signed on July 15th—the same day Andrey's citizenship papers were submitted and approved. An amazing journey. And yet it had barely begun.

I knew I would need help bringing Andrey home. My brother Brian agreed to meet us in Russia to assist. As a father to three boys, he was infinitely qualified to step in. I will always be indebted to him for this, especially as the schedule didn't go as planned and he ended up stranded by himself in an apartment in Moscow for days due to delays in the process.

The Journey Home

The flight home was long. With a fussy baby who didn't know me, who didn't understand what was happening, who had been removed from everything familiar, it was emotional and exhausting.

We landed at Newark Airport and processed through customs and immigration, where Andrey officially became a U.S. citizen. We continued to Reagan National Airport in DC, where dear friends met us—the beginning of an emotional support network that would sustain me through the next few years. Unknowingly at the time, I inadvertently changed the spelling of his name on his U.S. paperwork to Andrei. To me, he would always be Andrei. To him, as he grew and learned of his background and name, he would forever be Russian and Andrey.

Tired, jetlagged, exhilarated, I was grateful to see friendly faces to help me navigate home.

The next few days were a blur. Trying to settle into my home with a new addition. Hours of comforting and play, hoping Andrey would adjust to his new surroundings. Eventually he settled in, and we began a structured daily routine—so important for his adjustment to a new home, a new culture, a new mother.

I am grateful to my sister Caryn and her husband Chris for everything they did in those initial days and weeks. I was jetlagged, overwhelmed, and not sure what came next. I imagine this is what most new parents feel. It was just me, on my own, charting a new life course.

The Transformation

I took the next few months off from work to adjust to this new life. To help Andrey adjust to his. New home. New family. I couldn't even imagine what was going on in his brain, what sense he was making of this radical upheaval.

We spent two months with my mother at her house in Connecticut. This was a very special time for me and Andrey. The time with my mom was so helpful in transitioning into this new life. I loved every minute of it—in between the late nights, early mornings, and endless play. The time with my mom would become more important to both of us than I could have known then.

After a few months dedicated to new motherhood and Andrey's transition, I ventured back into the workplace. And I experienced what I imagine all parents—especially mothers—do when they return to work.

My attention was torn between home and work. I felt guilty leaving my baby with a caregiver. Guilty about not being able to focus on my work with the same intensity I once had. Yet somehow, it didn't matter as much anymore.

My priority had become my son. This was a strange transition for me. I had been so caught up in my career, in climbing the ladder, in proving myself. Now, suddenly, work felt different. Less urgent. Less central to my identity.

I struggled deeply with this shift. How could I continue to advance in my career while being a parent—a solo parent at that? Where should my priorities be? How would I know if I was getting the balance right? Was I failing at both by trying to do both?

The questions haunted me. I didn't have time to sit with them, to really work through what was happening. I was too busy just surviving—managing a job, caring for an infant, navigating the complexities of adoptive parenting, trying to hold it all together.

I was fortunate to have a wonderful team of people to carry on, who had been there during my absence and picked up the things that fell through the cracks of my divided attention. I felt the pressure of not being fully present anywhere—not at work, not at home.

The Cracks Begin to Show

Things came to a head later that year.

Another acquisition at my company. A new boss. Another challenge to my leadership, to my approach, to my value. At the time, I had no idea how all this stress was building up inside me. I was a new mother, learning to parent a child with special needs. I was navigating the corporate world as a single mother when most of my colleagues had spouses to share the load. I was trying to maintain the same level of performance and commitment that had defined my career while also being fully present for my son.

It was not sustainable. But I didn't know that yet. The stress was exacting a toll on my body, mind, and soul. But I was too busy, too committed, too determined to prove I could do it all to notice the warning signs.

The black sheep who had spent her life proving she was strong enough, smart enough, capable enough—she was about to learn the hardest lesson yet. That there are limits. That you can't do everything. That sometimes the strength to keep going looks less like perseverance and more like knowing when to stop.

That lesson was still ahead. Looking back now, I can see that adopting Andrey was the most important decision I ever made. Not just because it brought him into my life—though that alone would be enough—but because it forced me to become someone I had never been before.

I had spent my entire life in my head. Planning, strategizing, analyzing, thinking my way through problems. I had succeeded by being smart, by working hard, by proving myself through achievement.

You can't think your way through parenthood. You can't strategize your way through loving a child. You can't analyze your way to the kind of transformation that happens when you commit to another human being who needs you completely, who doesn't care about your credentials or your accomplishments or your carefully constructed identity.

Adopting Andrey required me to lead with my heart rather than my head. To make a decision based on connection rather than calculation. To embrace uncertainty rather than trying to control it. To be vulnerable in ways I had spent my entire life avoiding.

The girl who had grown up feeling like the black sheep, who had spent decades trying to prove she belonged, who had built a career on being different and smart and strategic—she had to become someone else. Someone softer. Someone more present. Someone who could hold a crying child at three in the morning and not worry about the morning meeting, who could be patient with developmental delays when patience had never been her strength, who could ask for help when independence had always been her armor.

This was leadership of a different kind. Not the strategic leadership I had practiced in my career, but something more fundamental: the leadership of showing up, day after day, for someone who needed me to be more than I thought I could be.

I didn't know it yet, but this leap of faith—this solo journey into motherhood—was preparing me for everything that would come after. The challenges of parenting a child with special needs. The reality of chronic illness. The ultimate breakdown that would force me to rebuild my life from the ground up.

Adopting Andrey broke me open. It shattered the carefully constructed persona I had built over decades. It revealed the limits of strategic thinking and meticulous planning. It showed me that the most important things in life can't be controlled or analyzed or thought through rationally.

Sometimes you just have to leap. Trust the connection. Follow your heart into territory your head says is too risky, too uncertain, too difficult.

The black sheep was becoming a mother. And in becoming a mother, she was finally, truly, becoming herself. The unexpected path had opened before me. And I had taken it, despite every rational reason not to.

What I didn't yet understand was just how unexpected this path would be. How much it would demand of me. How completely it would transform not just my life, but my understanding of leadership, resilience, strength, and what it means to be enough.

That understanding would come. In time. Through challenges I couldn't have anticipated. Through pain I couldn't have prepared for. Through transformation I couldn't have planned.

For now, I was simply a new mother, adjusting to a new life, trying to figure out how to be both the professional woman I had worked so hard to become and the mother I was learning to be.

The cracks were forming. The foundation was shifting. The breaking point was still ahead. But in this moment, holding my son, feeling the weight of him in my arms, seeing his bright blue eyes look up at me with trust I hadn't yet earned—in this moment, I was exactly where I needed to be.

The leap of faith had been taken. Now came the even harder part: living into what I had chosen.

CHAPTER 6

Redefining Motherhood

Little did I know, when I took the first step in adopting my son, what I was getting into.

But then, does any parent really know?

We imagine parenthood from the outside, constructing fantasies about what it will be like based on glimpses of other people's families, memories of our own childhoods, cultural narratives about motherhood that bear little resemblance to the messy reality. We think we're prepared because we've read the books, taken the classes, bought the equipment.

Then the child arrives, and all our preparation reveals itself as theoretical knowledge disconnected from lived experience.

For me, the gap between expectation and reality was particularly wide. I was a planner, a strategist, someone who succeeded by thinking things through thoroughly. I had spent my entire career mastering complexity through analysis and preparation.

Motherhood required something else entirely.

The Fundamental Shift

One of the first things I learned about being a parent is that your entire focus shifts from personal goals to raising your child. It's no longer about you. It's all about what you need to do to raise a person who will be kind and thrive in life.

This sounds obvious when stated plainly. Every parent knows this intellectually. But knowing it and living it are entirely different things.

I had to learn to let go of expectations—about what motherhood would look like, about what my child would be like, about what I would be like as a mother. I had to learn to parent by gut rather than by plan, to follow instincts I wasn't sure I possessed. I had to learn to put someone else first above all else, when I had spent my entire adult life prioritizing my career, my goals, my development.

For someone who lived in her head, who found safety in understanding and control, this was profoundly disorienting. I couldn't think my way through parenting. I couldn't strategize my way to being a good mother. I had to learn to flow, to adapt, to respond in the moment—all things that were deeply uncomfortable for a planner like me. But this fundamental shift became a crucial leadership lesson.

In learning to put my son first, in learning to serve his needs rather than impose my agenda, I was discovering something about leadership I had never fully understood in my professional life. The best leaders aren't the ones who control everything, who have all the answers, who impose their vision on others. The best leaders are the ones who serve—who help others grow, who create conditions for others to thrive, who subordinate their own needs to the needs of those they're leading.

This became a foundation of my leadership philosophy. Servant leadership—the idea that leadership is fundamentally about service rather than power—made intuitive sense to me once I experienced it in the most primal context possible: mothering a child.

But understanding this philosophically and embodying it practically while juggling the demands of solo motherhood and a career—that was another matter entirely.

The Solo Parent Reality

With any parent, there are challenges balancing career, family, and personal self-care. For a solo mom, the challenges expand exponentially.

You carry the entire burden of decision-making. There's no partner to consult, no one to share the weight of choosing schools, discipline approaches, medical treatments, financial priorities. Every choice rests on your shoulders alone. You carry the entire burden of childcare. There's no one to spell you when you're exhausted, no one to handle the morning routine while you get a few extra minutes of sleep, no one to manage bedtime while you catch up on work. You manage the household alone. The cooking, cleaning, laundry, repairs, yard work—all of it falls to you. There's no division of labor, no taking turns with the tedious tasks. You maintain financial security alone. One income, one job, one person's earning capacity to support two people. The pressure is constant.

It can be a lonely and exhausting place.

While family and friends were there to help out —and I was grateful for every bit of support— ultimately it all rested on my shoulders. I was the one who had to figure it out, manage it, carry it, sustain it, day after day, year after year.

The black sheep who had always prided herself on her independence discovered that being truly alone with the responsibility of raising a child was different from the independence she had cultivated in her career. This wasn't the empowering independence of choosing her own path. This was the isolating burden of having no one to share the weight.

There wasn't a lot written at the time about parenting adopted kids and the neurological issues many face. As is my nature, I spent an enormous amount of time researching the potential impacts of Andrei's challenging birth and early institutionalization.

Teenage pregnancy without adequate prenatal care. Breech birth. The impact of seizures during birth. Developmental and neurological issues arising from thirteen months in an orphanage environment. I read everything I could find, trying to understand what we might be facing, trying to prepare myself for what was coming.

I would come to understand over time just how fundamental these factors would be in Andrei's development and our lives together.

We joined FRUA—Families for Russian and Ukrainian Adoption—to connect with other adoptive parents. It was a wonderful resource on issues that commonly emerge in adoptive families. Each chapter held regular events: picnics, family gatherings, occasional experts speaking on adoption-related topics.

As a solo parent, a family of two, this was invaluable. It gave me a community of people who understood, who didn't judge, who were navigating similar challenges. It also gave me a window into some of the significant psychological, neurological, and physical issues that children adopted from Russia often face. Severe attachment disorder. Fetal alcohol spectrum disorder. Psychological issues related to identity and belonging.

I watched other families struggle with challenges far more severe than ours and felt both grateful and guilty. Grateful that Andrei's issues were relatively mild. Guilty for feeling relieved when I saw how much harder other families had it.

Andrei experienced mild attachment issues. For a long time, he was terrified to be alone, afraid that I would abandon him like everyone else in his short life had. He clung to me with a desperation that was both heartbreaking and exhausting.

This dissipated over time, though to this day he has a strong need to be around people. The fear of abandonment left its mark, even as he grew and healed.

I've always suspected mild fetal alcohol spectrum disorder, though he was never formally diagnosed. Alcohol use and abuse is common in Russian families. His birth mother—only fifteen when she conceived him, sixteen when she gave birth—reportedly met his birth father at a club, presumably where drinking took place. At least, that's what I was told by the staff at the baby house.

A medically difficult birth—breech, with a brief seizure—along with infections and illness in his early months, led to neurological issues and developmental delays that would shape his entire childhood and beyond.

Learning disabilities. Executive function deficits. Attention and working memory challenges. All of it stemming from those earliest experiences, long before I met him, beyond anyone's control.

A Different Path

Andrei and I are very different people. I live in my head. I plan things out meticulously and like to follow a plan. I find comfort in structure, in knowing what's coming, in having figured things out in advance. Andrei lives in the moment. He's spontaneous, creative, guided by feeling rather than planning. Structure constrains him. Plans feel restrictive. He knows what he needs intuitively, even when he can't articulate it.

I would learn over time to take Andrei's lead, to let him guide. He always knew what was best for him, even when my analytical mind thought I knew better. I often had to fight my own instincts about what I thought should happen and trust his instincts about what he needed.

This was perhaps the hardest lesson of motherhood for me: letting go of control, trusting someone else's knowledge, following rather than leading. We were charting a different path, the scope of which became more apparent over time. We were a different kind of family—a family of two. A mom, no dad.

The inevitable family tree exercise in preschool and kindergarten, designed to help children understand their place in the world, leads to questions and some confusion for non-traditional families. How do you explain a family with one parent, one grandparent, seemingly lopsided, populated with an aunt, an uncle and cousins and an unknown family across the world?

I tried different explanations as he grew. Some families have a mom and a dad. Some have two moms or two dads. Some, like ours, have just a mom. Family comes in many forms. What matters is love. I was always open with Andrei about his adoption and what I knew of his background and his family. And how much he meant to me. We had a favorite book - "The Best Single Mom in the World: How I Was Adopted." We celebrated Adoption Day each year, a milestone just like his birthday.

But explanations don't make it easier for a child who just wants to be like everyone else, who doesn't want to be different, who carries his own questions about why he was given up for adoption in the first place. The black sheep raising another black sheep, both of us learning to embrace being different while also longing to belong.

I was an older mom, often much older than the parents of his classmates. This left me feeling ostracized, excluded from the inevitable classroom and parent cliques. The other moms would gather for playdates and coffee, forming bonds I was rarely invited to share. Whether it was my age, my single status, or simply my own discomfort with social situations, I never quite fit into the parent community at his schools.

He was social and made friends easily, there were a plethora of birthday parties and holiday events. I involved myself in the parent community and took on leadership roles in the parent associations, perhaps hoping to make connections and lead in a different forum. I learned just how challenging this world is. It tested my mediation and collaboration skills. It also added to the emotional, mental and physical burden of being a solo mom, trying to balance a multitude of priorities.

The middle child who had never quite belonged, now the single adoptive mother who still didn't belong. The patterns run deep.

The Burden of Guilt

I carried perpetual guilt about not being enough of a mother. Not being able to give Andrei what he needed to develop and thrive.

These feelings are probably common to all parents, but they were exacerbated by the fact that there was only me to shoulder the responsibility of raising a neurodiverse child with special needs. And they tapped into the deep-seated insecurities of not being enough that I had learned in childhood, reinforced throughout my life.

I wasn't enough as a child, or at least so felt—not as smart as my sister, not as athletic, not as noticed. I wasn't enough as a professional—always having to prove myself, to work twice as hard, to justify my place. And now I wasn't enough as a mother—unable to give my son a father, unable to provide him with a two-parent home, unable to be both mother and father, unable to meet all his needs on my own.

The spiral of not-enough-ness was relentless.

I was wracked daily with the conflicts between my professional life and motherhood. My career took a backseat, which was excruciating for someone who had spent her entire life to that point building her professional persona and career identity. I felt this identity slip away over time as parenting responsibilities became paramount.

Who was I if not the strategic consultant, the health IT expert, the doctoral-educated professional? Who was I if I couldn't maintain the level of performance and commitment that had defined my career?

I sensed a shift in how I was viewed in the workplace. My schedule was bookended by school drop-off and pickup, a practice not always viewed favorably by colleagues—especially those without families, especially by my male colleagues with spouses who carried the household and childcare responsibilities.

I was no longer available for early morning meetings or evening work sessions. I couldn't travel as freely. I couldn't say yes to every opportunity. My attention was divided, my energy was finite, my priorities had shifted in ways that made me less valuable as an employee, even if I was becoming more valuable as a human being.

My priority became my family, and it strained my ability to lead the professional life I had always thought I would lead. I questioned how to fulfill my needs as a professional who had invested so much of herself in becoming the educated expert and leader I had aspired to be.

I often wondered if I had made the right decision to adopt—a thought I tried to quickly push aside. It plagued me, though, especially during times when I had to choose between work and my son, between my career ambitions and his needs, between who I had been and who I was becoming.

The Daily Reality

Every day was a flurry of activity.

Andrei was a night owl, so getting him up, organized, and out the door in the morning was a perpetual challenge. This is common with kids who have ADHD—trying to stay focused, keeping things organized despite all the distractions that pull at a child with executive function disorder.

The morning routine: wake him (multiple times). Coax him out of bed. Navigate the meltdown about what to wear. Guide him through breakfast without getting distracted by everything around him. Find the shoes. Find the backpack. Remember the homework. Get to the car. Get to school. By the time I dropped him off, I was already exhausted, and my workday hadn't even begun.

There was little time for myself. I tried to squeeze in the things that kept me grounded—running, walks in nature, cycling with Andrei in the trailer behind me. These weren't luxuries. They were necessities for maintaining some semblance of mental health, some connection to the person I had been before motherhood consumed everything.

But there was never enough time. Never enough energy. Never enough of me to go around.

Each summer, Andrei spent time at family camp in Maine with his aunt Caryn and her family. It was precious time for them to bond, time for him to connect with his cousins, to experience the kind of extended family that our little family of two couldn't provide on our own.

And it gave me a much-needed break. A week or two where I could catch up on work, sleep late, remember what it felt like to have time for myself.

It never seemed like enough. And yet, I always longed for him to come home. The house was so quiet when he wasn't there—something my introverted nature treasured while the mother in me just missed my son, missed the chaos and noise and constant demands of his presence.

Each year, we vacationed at the beach—sometimes Block Island, carrying on my family tradition, sometimes the Outer Banks of North Carolina. Our trips to Block Island often included my mom, giving them time to spend together, creating the connection I desperately wanted them to have.

We visited her in Connecticut regularly, multiple times a year. I wanted Andrei to be close to his grandmother, to bond over their common Russian heritage. But it became harder over time as Andrei grew older and my mom aged. Their personalities clashed, and I always thought it was because they were a lot alike.

The difference in ages created a gap that couldn't easily be filled.

The love was evident. The day-to-day challenges were immense. My mother had raised her children in a different era, with different expectations. She didn't always understand Andrei's needs or my parenting approaches. And Andrei, with his sensitivity and emotional needs, found her impatience and directness difficult to navigate.

I found myself in my familiar role of mediator, trying to bridge the gap between them, trying to make everyone happy, trying to create the family connection I thought we should have.

The middle child, still managing tensions, still trying to make it work.

DISCOVERING ANDREI

For all the challenges, there was also joy. Discovery. The delight of watching a person unfold.

Andrei didn't like to be alone. He didn't like the dark. He clung to "Beary" and "WoofWoof," his two favorite stuffed animals, with a ferocity that spoke to his need for something constant, something that wouldn't leave.

He had a soft spot for animals and collected stuffed animals wherever we went. They filled his bed, overflowed from his toy boxes, and populated his entire world. He had an active imagination, and his stuffed friends became his family. He would gather them around us for playtime and stories, creating elaborate scenarios, giving each one a voice and personality.

He loved arts and crafts—an instinct and talent we both worked to foster at home, at school, through art classes. This love of art would eventually lead him to his chosen career as an interior designer, though we didn't know that yet. We just knew that when he had paint and paper and materials to work with, something in him came alive.

He loved The Nutcracker. It became a tradition, one we maintain to this day, to see The Nutcracker every year at Christmas. First the local dance company versions for kids, and later, as he grew, at the Kennedy Center where we saw premier dance companies. We often came away with a new Nutcracker figurine to add to our growing collection.

As a child, he played with typical things—cars, train sets, toy kitchen. But he also loved dolls, an inclination not everyone in our world was comfortable with. I indulged it, defended it, insisted on his right to play with whatever called to him, even when other parents made comments or other children teased.

Let him be who he is, I thought. The world will try hard enough to make him conform. At least at home, he can be himself.

The black sheep mother, protecting her black sheep son, both of them learning that being different isn't something to be fixed.

He was quiet and shy until he warmed up to you. Then he was bright, funny, creative, affectionate—the sweetest child, according to every teacher who worked with him. They loved his kindness, his gentle nature, his easy-going demeanor despite the challenges he faced academically.

The early years of toddlerhood were quite joyful, despite the exhaustion. Andrei overcame some of the early developmental delays from spending thirteen formative months in an orphanage. When he came to his forever home, his language and growth were delayed, his body still catching up from birth complications, a sterile institutional environment, and less than optimal nutrition.

But children are resilient. With love, proper nutrition, stimulation, and security, he began to catch up. Not completely—the neurological impacts of his early experiences couldn't be entirely overcome. But enough. Enough to give us hope that he would be okay, that we would figure this out together.

We spent as much time as we could with family. Regular trips to my mom's took us on long road trips every month or two. Walks in the woods. Visits to the playground. Playtime with cousins building family ties that Andrei needed.

We were lucky to have a nanny for the first few years of Andrei's life in America—someone who loved him, who provided consistency and care while I worked. But when he turned three, it was time for preschool.

I never imagined how competitive preschool would be. Applications. Interviews. Play observations. Nail-biting anxiety waiting to hear whether he would get in.

Who would have thought entry to preschool would be a precursor to the college entry experience?

He got in. And at first, it went well. Andrei was extremely shy, just as I had been as a child. But his teachers loved him. He was a favorite for his kindness, his easy-going demeanor. He made friends, played hide and seek, and loved the playground. Always moving, always active.

His love of art began to emerge clearly. We spent hours on art projects and building things. I began to notice his talent for seeing a picture and bringing it to life, for understanding color and form and design in ways I never could.

THE WARNING SIGNS

The next year of preschool, the pressure ramped up. In a playful approach, they taught the alphabet and numbers, and began preparing the children for kindergarten.

The teachers began to notice things. Andrei had a hard time remembering things from week to week. He had difficulty staying focused. He reversed letters and numbers. He struggled to hold a pencil properly for any extended period.

Early signs of attention and working memory issues. Indications of dyslexia and dysgraphia. The neurological impacts of his early experiences manifested in concrete, observable ways.

I tried not to panic. Early childhood development happens at different rates, I told myself. He'll catch up. He just needs more time.

But a part of me knew. A part of me had been preparing for this since the day I first learned about his medical history. The difficult birth, the seizures, the orphanage stay—it all had consequences that would follow him through childhood and beyond.

We were entering new territory. Not just parenting, but parenting a child whose brain worked in different ways than others. Not just managing my career and family, but advocating for a child who would need extra support, extra services, extra patience from systems not designed for children like him.

In the end, it all took a toll on my physical health, my mental health, my emotional health.

Every day was a battle with time. Rushing to school drop-off. Rushing to work. Rushing to complete ten hours of work in six hours so I could pick up Andrei after school for the innumerable appointments—speech therapy, occupational therapy, developmental assessments, IEP meetings.

Squeezing my career into the margins, managing my team remotely, trying to maintain the level of expertise and strategic thinking that had defined my professional identity while also being fully present for a child who needed so much from me.

I was running on fumes, sustained by adrenaline and sheer determination. I told myself I could handle it. I told myself this was what motherhood required, what single parenthood demanded, what I had signed up for when I made the decision to adopt.

Handling it and thriving are not the same thing though. I was handling it. Barely. At great cost. And the costs were accumulating in ways I couldn't yet see.

The perfectionist who had always demanded excellence from herself was now demanding it in two separate, equally demanding roles: professional and mother. Neither could be done halfway. Both required everything.

Something was going to break. I just didn't know yet what it would be.

Redefining Success

Motherhood forced me to redefine what success meant.

In my career, success had been measurable: degrees earned, positions achieved, projects completed, clients satisfied. I could point to accomplishments, put them on a resume, and demonstrate my value through concrete outputs.

Motherhood offered no such clarity. What did it mean to be a successful mother, specially a single mother of a child with a neurodiverse child?

Was it about his happiness? His development? His eventual independence? Was it about giving him a stable home, a loving environment, opportunities to thrive? How would I know if I was succeeding or failing?

There were no clear metrics, no performance reviews, no objective measures. Just the day-to-day grind of showing up, making decisions, hoping for the best, second-guessing everything.

And through it all, trying to hold onto some sense of myself—the woman I had been before motherhood, the professional I still wanted to be, the person who existed beyond the role of mother.

That integration was proving harder than I ever imagined. The personal and professional were not complementary aspects of a whole self. They were competing demands, pulling me in opposite directions, requiring different versions of myself that couldn't coexist comfortably.

The black sheep who had spent her life proving she could do things her own way was discovering that doing it your own way—solo motherhood plus demanding career—came at a cost she hadn't fully calculated.

The lessons about servant leadership, about putting others first, about adapting rather than controlling—these were profound and valuable. They were changing how I understood leadership, how I showed up in my work, how I related to the world.

But those lessons weren't making it easier. If anything, they were making it harder, because I now understood what it truly meant to give everything, and I could see that I was trying to give everything to two different, equally demanding parts of my life.

Something would have to give.

But not yet. For now, I was still trying to be everything to everyone. Still trying to prove I could do it all. Still running, both literally and metaphorically, from the fear that I wasn't enough.

The cracks were widening. The foundation was shifting. The breaking point was getting closer. There were still lessons to learn, still challenges to face, still ways in which this journey into motherhood would transform and prepare me for what was coming. The unexpected path continued to unfold. And I continued to walk it, one exhausting, precious, impossible day at a time.

CHAPTER 7

Navigating Different Minds

There is a parallel universe of education that most people don't know about, unless you're in it.

You may have heard of special education. You probably have some thoughts about what it means. You may know someone with a child in the special education system and believe you understand what that entails.

Let me assure you: you don't. Not really. Unless you have experienced the system yourself, either as a student or as a parent of a child receiving special education services, it remains fundamentally opaque. It's a world unto itself, with its own language, its own rules, its own bureaucracy, its own unwritten codes that you only learn through bitter experience.

I didn't know this world existed until I had no choice but to enter it. And once you enter, you can never fully leave. It becomes a permanent part of your reality, a lens through which you see education, childhood development, systems of support and neglect, equity and injustice.

It changes everything.

The Early Signs

The journey into this world started when Andrei was four or five. In reality, it probably started earlier. I just didn't recognize the signs.

For many families, it takes years for learning challenges to become apparent. The child seems fine in the early years, then struggles emerge in second or third grade when academic demands increase. By then, they've fallen behind, and catching up is harder.

For others, the signs are noticeable early on. It was this way with Andrei.

Once he started preschool, the learning differences became clear. There was the acute shyness and reluctance to fully engage. Hesitance to respond to questions, to offer input when asked. Difficulty staying focused on tasks that required sustained attention.

His handwriting was illegible—not just messy in the way all young children's handwriting is messy, but truly indecipherable, the letters malformed and inconsistent.

He had difficulty coming up with the right words at the right time. You could see him searching, reaching for language that remained just out of grasp. Letters and numbers appeared reversed on the page. He struggled to remember what was taught the day before, the lesson vanishing from his mind as if it had never been there. I sometimes wondered if some of this was related to his early life in Russia. How much of the Russian language did he learn and retain? Was his brain trying to translate from Russian, his first language, to English, his now second language? As a teen, he taught himself to speak Russian, with the help of a friend. He picked it up easily and is now fluent in the language.

In general, there were challenges with recall—experiences, events, facts. They didn't stick in his memory the way they should. Difficulty expressing feelings and emotions, needs and wants. And with the recognition that he was different from the other children, extreme frustration began to set in, along with feelings of being "less than."

I watched him struggle. I watched other children master skills that eluded him. I watched him try so hard and still fall short. And my heart broke a little more each time.

He began to fall behind very early in the year before entering kindergarten. The teachers recommended psychological testing—a battery of assessments designed to map cognitive processing, working memory, executive functioning, attention profiles, and language development.

The first time he was tested, he was five years old.

He would undergo testing regularly over the years, every few years, always with similar results. Eventually, he was tested by a neuropsychologist with an even more extensive battery of tests, required to receive special educational services in the public school system.

A portfolio of diagnoses came back, all indicating a neurodiversity:

ADHD: Attention Deficit Hyperactivity Disorder: The difficulty focusing, the constant movement, the impulsivity.

Dyslexia: difficulty with reading, with decoding written language, with the fundamental skill our entire educational system is built upon.

Dysgraphia: difficulty with writing, with the physical act of forming letters, with getting thoughts from brain to paper.

Auditory processing disorder: difficulty processing and making sense of sounds, which affects everything from following directions to learning phonics to participating in classroom discussions.

Language processing disorder: difficulty with receptive and expressive language, with understanding what's said and articulating responses.

Working memory disorder: difficulty holding information in mind long enough to use it, which affects everything from following multi-step directions to doing mental math to completing complex tasks.

A constellation of overlapping traits, all stemming from the same source: the neurological impacts of his difficult birth and the sterile environment of an orphanage that offered little in the way of developmental enrichment.

These conditions are now known to inhibit brain and neurological development, leading to exactly the types of challenges Andrei was facing. The science confirms what I had suspected from the beginning—that those first thirteen months of his life had shaped his brain in ways that would affect him forever.

On one hand, being able to put names to what we were seeing was reassuring. There were reasons for his struggles. Explanations. A framework for understanding.

On the other hand, it was overwhelming. These weren't temporary delays he would outgrow. These were permanent neurological differences he would navigate for the rest of his life. The challenges wouldn't disappear. At best, he would learn strategies to compensate, accommodations to work around his differences, ways to succeed despite a brain that processed information differently from the norm.

At this point, I took on a new role: advocate, in addition to my role as solo parent.

My world changed in that instant.

Entering the System

Because Andrei was in a private school—recommended by all the psychologists who tested him—we didn't immediately enter the public school special education system.

His early education, from kindergarten through elementary and middle school, took place in specialized schools specifically designed to educate children with extensive learning differences. Small class sizes, teachers trained in multisensory instruction, curricula adapted to different learning styles, environments structured to support executive function challenges.

These schools understood neurodiversity. They expected it, accommodated it, worked with it rather than against it.

But they were private. And private meant expensive. Tuition that consumed a significant portion of my salary, that required constant financial juggling, that limited other options and opportunities. This was the trade-off: quality specialized education in exchange for financial strain that never let up.

One foray into the public school system in fourth grade was a disaster.

I thought we could make it work. We had an Individual Education Plan—an IEP, the legal document that outlines special education services and accommodations. The school was required by law to provide the services specified in the IEP. It should have worked.

It didn't.

Even with the IEP approved, the services did not meet expectations and were not readily available as promised. The classroom support he needed didn't materialize. The accommodations weren't consistently implemented. The specialized instruction was generic at best. When things started to fall apart, when it became clear he wasn't getting what he needed, I requested a meeting with the special education case manager.

It took four weeks to get that meeting scheduled. Four weeks of watching my son struggle. Four weeks of him falling further behind. Four weeks of frustration building, anxiety increasing, his sense of being "less than" intensifying.

This was an untenable situation. We left and returned to a private specialized school within three months.

The lesson was clear: the public system, at least in our district, was not equipped to serve children like Andrei. Not because of bad intentions, but because of insufficient resources, inadequate training, overwhelming caseloads, and a bureaucracy that moved at a pace divorced from the reality of a child's daily experience in a classroom where they're drowning.

The Trade-offs

There are pros and cons to specialized private education.

The pros: Generally high-quality instruction with administrators and teachers trained in teaching to different learning styles. Greater appreciation for and ability to tailor lessons to specific needs. Small class sizes where no child gets lost. An environment designed around the assumption of difference rather than the expectation of conformity.

The cons: Costly tuition that strains family finances. Sets a track of independent schools for the entirety of elementary and secondary education—once you're in this parallel system, it's hard to exit. Different social norms from mainstream schools, which can make the transition to college or work harder. Friend circles that form outside normal school-based social systems, which means your child's friends aren't your neighbors' children, aren't the kids on your street. No access to school-based extracurricular activities—no football team, no marching band, no school plays. Enormous strain on families, especially working parents who have to manage drop-offs and pickups and schedules that don't align with typical work hours.

Every choice was a trade-off. There was no perfect option, no solution that addressed all needs. Just a series of decisions about which challenges we could live with and which we couldn't.

I became adept at weighing options, at evaluating systems, at making strategic decisions with incomplete information—all skills I used in my professional life, now applied to the most personal domain possible.

The systems thinker, analyzing the complex adaptive system of special education, trying to navigate it effectively for my son.

Outside of school, the day-to-day of parenting a neurodiverse child requires an enormous amount of patience, creativity, and persistence.

Mornings involve struggles with transitions—a hallmark of executive functioning differences. Moving from sleeping to waking, from waking to getting out of bed, from pajamas to clothes, from house to car, from car to school—each transition a potential battleground, each requiring negotiation and support.

What seems simple to a neurotypical person—a series of straightforward steps in a logical sequence—becomes a complex challenge for someone with executive function deficits. The brain that struggles to plan, initiate, and sequence actions needs external support for what others do automatically.

Homework time requires inventive strategies. Movement breaks every fifteen minutes. Dictation instead of handwriting when the physical act of writing becomes too frustrating. Graphic organizers instead of blank pages, providing structure when the brain struggles to generate its own organizational systems.

Reading becomes a shared endeavor. Audiobooks that allow him to access stories without the struggle of decoding text. Multisensory tools—highlighting, color-coding, manipulatives—that bridge the gap between interest and skill.

Everything takes longer. Everything requires more support. Everything demands more energy—from him and from me.

And through it all, I'm watching him work so much harder than other children to achieve less. I'm watching him put in twice the effort for half the result. I'm watching him internalize the message that he's not good enough, that something is wrong with him, that he's broken in some fundamental way.

That last part—watching him absorb society's judgments about his worth—that's the hardest part of all.

Reframing Difference

Over time, I came to understand different ways of learning, of engaging with the world, of making meaning from experience.

Rather than looking at Andrei's learning challenges as disabilities—as our educational system labels them—I came to see them as differences. Not deficits, but divergences. Not problems to be fixed, but variations in how human brains can be wired.

Raising a neurodiverse child teaches you to see cognitive diversity not as an exception but as a fundamental feature of being human. Neurotypical is just one way a brain can work, not the only correct way, not the standard against which all others should be measured and found wanting.

Patterns emerge when you pay attention. Divergent thinking—the ability to see multiple solutions, to make unexpected connections, to approach problems from angles others miss. High creativity—the capacity to imagine, to design, to create beauty. Bursts of hyperfocus—deep immersion in topics of interest, the ability to sustain attention for hours when something captures the imagination. Nonlinear problem-solving—getting to solutions through unexpected routes, finding answers that linear thinkers would never discover. Sensory sensitivities—experiencing the world more intensely, noticing details others overlook.

You begin appreciating not only the challenges but the strengths that accompany neurological differences.

Andrei's visual-spatial intelligence, his ability to see in three dimensions, to understand how colors and shapes and forms work together—these weren't separate from his dyslexia. They were part of the same neurological wiring that made reading difficult but design intuitive.

His creativity, his imagination, his ability to think outside conventional boxes—these weren't despite his ADHD. They were expressions of a brain that didn't default to linear, sequential, rule-bound thinking.

His empathy, his emotional sensitivity, his attunement to others' feelings—these weren't unrelated to his language processing challenges. They were part of a person who experienced the world through feeling as much as through words.

The disability framework focuses on deficits, on what's missing or broken or wrong. But what if we asked different questions? What if we noticed what's present, what's strong, what's different in ways that could be valuable if we built environments that appreciated those differences?

I was learning to see my son not as a collection of disorders to be treated, but as a whole person whose brain worked beautifully—just differently.

Parenting a neurodiverse child requires resilience. Not just the resilience of pushing through adversity, of gritting your teeth and persevering despite difficulties though.

It requires reflective resilience—the capacity to adapt, to learn, to persist while also changing course when something isn't working. The wisdom to know when to push and when to pivot. The flexibility to let go of expectations and meet the child you have rather than the child you imagined.

It's resilience in the face of repeated disappointments. Schools that promise support but don't deliver. Therapies that work for a while then plateau. Strategies that help with one challenge but create others. Progress that comes slower than you hoped, in smaller increments than you expected.

It's resilience in the face of judgment. From other parents who think you're making excuses for bad behavior or lack of discipline. From family members who think he just needs to try harder. From strangers who have opinions about parenting choices they don't understand. From systems that view difference as deficit and disability as personal failure.

It's resilience in the face of your own limitations. The times you lose patience. The times you can't figure out what he needs. The times you make the wrong call, choose the wrong school, implement the wrong strategy. The times you're simply too exhausted to be the parent he deserves.

It's also the resilience of pushing through tough times to see the glimmers shine through in the best moments. Watching your child emerge as a unique person whose differences are the core of their creative light in the world. Teaching them to advocate for themselves, to see their differences as positive, to claim their place in a world that often doesn't make space for them.

Every small victory becomes monumental. The first time he reads a sentence independently. The first time he completes homework without tears. The first time he asks for what he needs. The first time he stands up for himself. The first time he creates something beautiful and knows it's beautiful.

These moments sustain you. They remind you why you fight so hard, why you don't give up, why you keep advocating and supporting and believing when the world sends messages that you shouldn't.

The Social Cost

Socially, it's not easy being neurodiverse. Being different. Thinking in a different way. Seeing the world in a different way.

Andrei is a social soul—he needs people, craves connection, wants to belong. But neurodiversity often makes belonging harder. I watched over time as his best friends became strangers, as they moved on from him as they grew up. Children are developing their own identities, forming their own social hierarchies, and often the different kid gets left behind.

It wasn't that anyone was cruel to him. It was more subtle than that. Invitations that stopped coming. Playdates that became less frequent and then stopped altogether. Friend groups that formed around activities or interests he couldn't fully participate in. The slow, quiet drift of children who were once close becoming acquaintances and then strangers.

Outwardly, he took it in stride. He didn't complain. He didn't demand explanations. He simply accepted that this was how things were. But inwardly, I could see a lot of pain under the surface, tucked away in a box of buried emotion. The hurt of being left out. The confusion about why friendships ended. The growing sense that something about him made him less desirable as a friend.

I wanted to fix it. I wanted to force other children to see his worth, to appreciate his kindness and creativity and gentle spirit. I wanted to protect him from the social consequences of being different.

I couldn't. This was part of what neurodiversity meant in our society—not just struggling with academics, but struggling to fit into social structures built for brains that work differently from his.

All I could do was be there. Listen when he wants to talk. Hold space for feelings he couldn't articulate. Model for him that being different isn't being less. Keep reinforcing that the right people would see his value, even if others didn't.

The middle child who had felt left out, not quite fitting in, now watching her son experience similar isolation. The patterns repeating across generations, different manifestations of the same core experience.

Systems Thinking, Personal Edition

My professional work had always involved systems thinking—understanding how complex adaptive systems function, how changes in one part ripple through the whole, how emergence happens through interaction rather than central control.

Now I was applying that systems thinking to education, to neurodiversity, to my own family system.

I began to see how the special education system was designed around efficiency and standardization rather than individualization and support. How funding structures created incentives that didn't align with student needs. How teacher training programs prepared educators for classrooms of neurotypical children and left them unprepared for the diversity they would actually encounter. How testing and accountability measures punished schools for students who learned differently. How the entire structure was built on assumptions about typical development that excluded or pathologized significant portions of the population.

This wasn't about bad people making bad choices. This was about system design, about incentive structures, about what gets measured and valued. About how bureaucracies function and how they resist change even when change is desperately needed.

Understanding the system didn't make navigating it easier. But it did help me see where the leverage points were, where advocacy might be effective, where I was fighting against individual people versus fighting against structural barriers beyond any individual's control.

It enhanced my systemic thinking in my professional work. It made me a better consultant, better at seeing patterns, better at understanding how organizational systems function and dysfunction. Better at helping clients see the invisible structures shaping outcomes they thought were about individual performance or effort.

My personal struggle was deepening my professional capacity. The two domains of my life that had felt so separate, so in conflict, were actually feeding each other in ways I couldn't have predicted.

The black sheep who had always seen things differently now had a son who literally saw things differently. Together, we were learning to navigate a world not built for either of us. And in that navigation, I was becoming someone I had never expected to be.

Not just a mother. Not just a professional. But someone who understood at a bone-deep level what it meant to be different, to not fit, to have to fight for space in systems designed for other people.

Someone who could hold both the suffering and the gifts that come with difference. Who could see the beauty in brains that work differently while also acknowledging the very real challenges those brains face in a world that demands conformity.

Someone whose empathy, hard-won through her own experiences of being the black sheep, now extended to her black sheep son and to all the other children and families navigating this parallel universe of special education that most people never see.

The teacher who appeared when the student was ready. The student who appeared when the teacher was ready. In this case, the student and teacher were the same person, learning from her son what she needed to know not just for him, but for herself.

The journey through special education wasn't linear. There were good years and hard years, progress and setbacks, victories and defeats.

There were IEP meetings where I had to fight for every accommodation, every service, every modification—learning to be fierce in a system that preferred compliant parents who didn't question or challenge. Learning the language, the laws, the regulations that gave me leverage. Learning when to collaborate and when to demand. Learning to document everything, to assume nothing, to verify that promises became actual implementation.

There were evaluations and reevaluations, testing and retesting, always trying to understand exactly where Andrei was developmentally, cognitively, academically. Always trying to identify what he needed next, what support would help, what strategies might work.

There were transitions—from preschool to elementary, elementary to middle school, middle school to high school. Each transition required new planning, new advocacy, new efforts to make sure support carried over, that information was communicated, that he didn't fall through the cracks that open up between educational levels.

There were therapies—speech therapy, occupational therapy, educational therapy, social skills groups. So many appointments, so many hours sitting in waiting rooms, so many copays, so much time management to fit everything in around school and work.

And through it all, there was Andrei. Growing, developing, becoming himself. Not in spite of his neurodiversity but through it, because of it, as an inseparable part of it.

The boy who couldn't read well but could see how spaces should be designed. The boy who never reads but who could intuitively build and construct things, the boy who struggled to remember facts but never forgot kindness. The boy who processed language differently but understood emotion deeply.

My son. My teacher. My invitation to see the world differently.

The journey into the parallel universe of special education transformed me as much as it challenged me. It gave me new skills, new perspectives, new capacities. It connected my professional expertise with my personal experience in ways that enriched both.

It also exhausted me. Depleted me. Pushed me toward a breaking point I was still trying to avoid seeing.

Because this journey, as profound and transformative as it was, was still just one dimension of a life that was becoming increasingly unsustainable. The special education advocacy was layered on top of solo parenting, which was layered on top of a demanding career, which was all built on a foundation of trying to be perfect at everything, trying to prove I was enough, trying to hold it all together through sheer force of will.

Something was going to break. The cracks were spreading. The foundation was crumbling.

But not yet. For now, I was still fighting. Still advocating. I'm still learning. Still growing. Still trying to be everything to everyone while slowly losing myself in the process. The unexpected path continued to wind through territory I had never imagined. And I continued to walk it, one difficult, instructive, impossible step at a time.

CHAPTER 8

When the Body Rebels

When I was first diagnosed with chronic myeloid leukemia, I was already drowning.

I was juggling solo parenthood in all its complexity. I had just started a new job. My schedule was crushing: getting out of the house in the morning, managing school drop-off and pickup, cobbling together afterschool activities when I could squeeze them in. Learning the ropes at a new company, building a team, meeting with clients, always with an eye on the clock.

Every day pushed me to the limit of exhaustion with little time to recoup—something I knew I needed to stay grounded but could never quite find. So when a routine visit to my doctor showed a wildly high white blood cell count, I could see the muted alarm in her reaction.

She tried to keep her voice neutral, professional. But I caught it—the slight pause, the way her eyes moved from the lab results to my face, the shift in her demeanor from routine to concern.

"I'm going to refer you to a hematologist," she said. "Right away."

That was all I needed to hear to know something was seriously wrong.

THE DIAGNOSIS

Repeated tests showed continually rising levels of white blood cells—a sign of leukemia, though they wouldn't confirm it yet. Then came the bone marrow biopsy, a procedure as unpleasant as it sounds, extracting samples from the center of my hip bone for DNA testing.

This took place just as we were scheduled to leave on a short getaway. A brief escape, a chance to breathe, just me and Andrei spending time together away from the grind of daily life.

It was a tense time. I could feel the anxiety and fear of what the future might hold building inside me, tightening around my chest like a vise. Questions I couldn't answer. Scenarios I couldn't stop imagining. A future suddenly uncertain in ways it had never been before.

Yet I could not share this with anyone. I certainly couldn't share it with my four-year-old son, still working through attachment anxiety, still afraid that I would abandon him like his birth mother had. How could I tell him that his mother—the only parent he had, the one constant in his life—might be seriously ill?

And in typical form, I kept it all inside to deal with on my own until I knew what we were facing, until I could process the results and figure out what it meant. The black sheep, once again handling everything alone, not knowing how to ask for help, not trusting that help would come if she did.

I was on pins and needles the entire trip. Waiting for test results. Trying to be present for

Andrei while my mind spun through worst-case scenarios. Smiling and playing and pretending everything was fine while terror churned beneath the surface.

When the call came from the hematologist —"Can you come to the office as soon as you get back home?"—my anxiety spiked even higher. Just a request. No results provided over the phone. Just the ominous summons to come in.

I went in as soon as we returned.

"You have Chronic Myeloid Leukemia," the hematologist said. "CML. It's a chronic form of leukemia caused by a chromosomal mutation."

The word "leukemia" hit me like a physical blow. Cancer. I had cancer. At forty-something, as a single mother with a young child who needed me.

I tried to hide my alarm, to stay calm and present, to absorb the information rationally. But my mind was already racing ahead. How long did I have? What was the prognosis? How would Andrei survive if something happened to me?

Then came the part that saved me.

"The good news," the doctor continued, "is that what once required nauseating chemotherapy drugs, a bone marrow transplant, or both—with uncertain life expectancy—has changed dramatically in recent years. A new drug called Gleevec became available just five years ago, and the response rates are astounding. For most patients, it essentially turns a deadly cancer into a manageable chronic condition."

I felt something in my chest loosen slightly. Not relief, exactly. But a shift from pure terror to cautious hope.

"We'll start you on Gleevec immediately," he said. "Most patients respond very well."

The Treatment

I started the medication that week. One pill a day. That was it. One pill standing between me and the progression of cancer.

The waiting began again. Would I be one of the patients who responded? Would the drug work? How quickly would we know?

Within six months, the indicators of chromosomal abnormality were less than one percent. Effectively in remission. The cancer was still there—the mutation in my chromosomes couldn't be erased—but it was controlled, suppressed, kept from progressing.

I could breathe again. It changed me though. I viewed life differently. More precarious, more valued. The people in my life became more treasured, some things mattered less.

I settled into a pattern of six-month visits to the oncologist, each time with the same positive results. The remission was holding. The drug was working.

I was lucky. I had virtually no side effects—just some mild nausea when taking my daily dose of Gleevec, easily managed by taking it with food. For many cancer patients, treatment is nearly as debilitating as the disease itself. For me, it was a miracle cure.

But miracles come with price tags.

A month's supply of Gleevec costs over ten thousand dollars.

Ten. Thousand. Dollars. Every month. For the rest of my life.

Without insurance, I couldn't afford to survive. The medication that stood between me and death was priced beyond the reach of most people who needed it.

I had insurance through my employer, so the copay was manageable. This fact—this absolute dependence on employer-sponsored health insurance—would guide many decisions I would make over the ensuing years.

I couldn't quit a job I didn't like without securing other employment first. I couldn't take a break, couldn't freelance, couldn't do anything that would risk losing access to insurance. I was trapped by the economics of staying alive, by the American healthcare system that ties survival to employment status.

The strategic thinker in me understood the systemic issues. The health policy expert in me knew all about the problems with our insurance-based healthcare model. Understanding it intellectually didn't make it less terrifying to live within its constraints.

The mother in me just knew: I have to stay alive for Andrei. And staying alive means keeping this job, no matter what. No matter how exhausting. No matter how unsustainable. No matter what toll it takes.

Another constraint added to a life already running at maximum capacity with no margin for error.

The Secret

I couldn't share any of this with Andrei. Not yet. Maybe not for years.

I was afraid it would shatter the fragile attachment we had been building. He was still working through his abandonment trauma, still learning to trust that I wouldn't leave him. How could I tell him that I had a disease, that I was taking medication every day to stay alive, that there was even a possibility—however remote—that I might not always be there?

I couldn't take that risk.

So I lived with a secret. Pills hidden in the medicine cabinet. Doctor's appointments scheduled on days when he was at school. Medical forms and insurance statements tucked away where he wouldn't see them.

A double life, in a way. Always on guard, always careful not to let my concerns and fears show up at the wrong time, in a way that would upset the fine balance of the life I had worked so hard to create.

It was years before I would even broach the subject with him. Years of carrying this alone.

I lived with my fears bottled up inside. Fears of not being able to take care of him. Fears of abandoning him just as he was learning to trust that

I would never leave. Fears of acute relapse, of treatment failure, of running out of time.

The weight of it all pressed down on me constantly. But I kept moving, kept functioning, kept pretending everything was fine.

Well-meaning people encouraged me to be vulnerable, to share my situation with others. "You don't have to carry this alone," they said. "Let people help you."

This was hard for me. Vulnerability had never been my strength. I was the competent one, the capable one, the one who handled things. Asking for help felt like admitting weakness, like proving I wasn't as strong as I needed to be.

But I tried.

I confided in my family. That was easy—they were family, they loved me unconditionally, they would be there no matter what. My mother, my sister, my brother—they provided support and reassurance without judgment.

I shared with coworkers I thought would be empathetic, who would have my back. Most did, and I was grateful for their support. They checked in on me, offered flexibility when I needed it, and held space for what I was going through.

But some took the opportunity to undermine me. To use my vulnerability against me, to suggest that maybe I couldn't handle the responsibilities of the role, to position themselves as more reliable alternatives. Cancer became ammunition in workplace politics I hadn't anticipated.

It took a toll. I became more cautious about trusting others. I closed off parts of myself I had just been learning to open. The lesson reinforced what I had always suspected: showing vulnerability invites exploitation. Better to handle things on my own.

The times I did ask for help, I often felt disappointed. People's support was contingent, limited, and unreliable. It only steeled my resolve to handle things myself, to not count on anyone, to prove I could do it all despite the cancer, despite the single parenthood, despite everything.

The pressure continued to build.

Learning to Live with It

Eventually, I was able to move on from the day-to-day fear that I would get acutely sick and there would be no one to take care of Andrei.

Once I learned that my cancer was in remission and remained in remission over months and then years, I was able to reset my thinking. This wasn't a death sentence. This was a chronic illness managed by medication. I would have to take a pill every day for the rest of my life. I would have to see an oncologist twice a year. I would have to remain vigilant, watching for signs of relapse.

But I could live. I could parent. I could work. I could build a life.

The acute terror faded into something more manageable—a background hum of anxiety, always present but not constantly overwhelming. Only occasionally would I be led to the brink of "what ifs," spiraling into worst-case scenarios before pulling myself back to the present reality: I was fine.

The medication was working. I was going to be okay.

I guess this is what resilience looks like.

Not the absence of fear. Not heroic triumph over adversity. Just the daily practice of moving forward despite uncertainty. Of functioning despite chronic stress. Of holding both the reality of illness and the possibility of a full life.

I would have many opportunities in the next few years to know and practice the tools of resilience. More than I wanted. More than I thought I could handle.

A consummate planner who always had a goal, I began to appreciate the value of taking life a day at a time. I learned through this experience that we never know the twists and turns life will take, that sometimes the best we can do is believe that things will work out.

A positive attitude and an adaptable approach go a long way toward navigating the uncertainties of chronic illness, parenthood, and neurodiversity. But these lessons, however valuable, came at a cost.

The Question of Causation

As I learned more about CML and the chromosomal aberrations that cause it, I couldn't help but wonder: Had chronic stress contributed to this?

The more I learned about the effects of stress on the body—particularly a state of chronic stress over time—the more convinced I became that there was a connection.

Chronic stress affects every system in the body. It dysregulates the immune system, creates inflammation, disrupts cellular processes. It's associated with increased cancer risk, autoimmune disorders, cardiovascular disease. The body under sustained stress begins to break down in predictable ways.

And I had been under sustained stress for years. The pressure of my career, the demands of solo parenting, the financial strain, the constant juggling, the perfectionism that demanded excellence in every domain, the inability to rest, the lack of support, the isolation.

My body had been sending me signals for a while. The exhaustion that never lifted. The tension I carried in my shoulders and neck. The trouble sleeping despite being chronically tired. The way my heart would race at the slightest provocation. The headaches. The digestive issues. The sense of being wound too tight, always on edge, never able to fully relax.

I had ignored all of it. Pushed through. Told myself I was fine, I could handle it, I just needed to work harder.

And now my body was rebelling in a way I couldn't ignore. The chromosomal mutation that caused CML was random, the doctors told me. Bad luck. Not my fault. Nothing I did or didn't do. But I wondered. I still wonder. How much does the body absorb before it breaks? How much chronic stress can we sustain before something fundamental gives way?

I couldn't prove causation. But I couldn't shake the conviction that the way I had been living—the relentless pace, the impossible demands, the refusal to acknowledge limits—had contributed to my body's breakdown.

The Impossible Balancing Act

This experience made me more conscious of the need to take care of myself. To prioritize rest, to manage stress, to build in recovery time, to create some kind of sustainable rhythm.

As a solo mom, there was never enough time for the restorative, recuperative practices I needed. There was nowhere to retreat when the demands of parenthood and professional responsibilities collided. No partner to spell me so I could rest. No backup when I was depleted. No margin for being anything less than fully functional.

I needed to slow down. But slowing down meant failing at something—being a less attentive mother, a less committed employee, a less ambitious professional. The perfectionist in me couldn't accept that. The woman who had spent her life proving she was enough couldn't admit she had reached her limits.

So I kept going. Taking my pill every day. Showing up for work. Taking care of Andrei. Maintaining the appearance of having it all under control.

The cancer was in remission, but the conditions that may have contributed to it—the chronic stress, the unsustainable pace, the perfectionism, the isolation—remained unchanged.

I was treating the symptom while ignoring the underlying cause.

During this time, I was also just beginning to discover the full extent of Andrei's neurodiversity. He had just started his second year of preschool, and his learning challenges were starting to emerge more clearly. He loved learning and going to school. He loved his teachers and the friends he made. He was finally coming out of his shell, showing his fun-loving personality.

But he was struggling to keep up with the pace of learning. This would become a pattern over the next few years—periods of apparent progress followed by plateaus or regressions as new demands exceeded his capacity.

It was the beginning of my introduction into the world of special education, of neuropsychological testing and evaluations that would become a regular part of our lives.

So now I was managing: a demanding new job, solo parenting, a cancer diagnosis and daily medication, regular oncology appointments, emerging recognition of my son's special needs, and the beginning of what would be years of educational advocacy and special services coordination.

Each challenge on its own would have been significant. Together, they created a load that was objectively unsustainable. But I didn't know how to stop. I didn't know how to ask for help effectively. I didn't know how to admit I couldn't handle it all.

The black sheep who had always done things her own way was trapped in a pattern of her own making. Proving her strength by refusing to acknowledge weakness. Demonstrating her capability by taking on more than any one person could reasonably manage. Justifying her worth by being indispensable, by never faltering, by handling impossible challenges with apparent ease.

The body keeps score, though. It tracks every stress, every exhaustion, every moment of pushing beyond sustainable limits. And eventually, the bill comes due.

For me, it came in the form of chromosomal mutation and cancer cells proliferating in my bone marrow. The warning shot had been fired. But I wasn't yet ready to receive the message.

Lessons in Vulnerability and Strength

There's a particular kind of strength that chronic illness teaches.

It's not the strength of pushing through, of ignoring pain, of powering past obstacles through sheer determination. That's the strength I had always relied on—the perfectionist's strength, the achiever's strength, the black sheep's strength of proving herself against all odds.

Chronic illness teaches a different kind of strength: the strength of acknowledging limits. The strength of accepting help. The strength of adapting rather than controlling. The strength of living with uncertainty, with vulnerability, with the knowledge that you are not invincible.

I was learning this strength slowly, reluctantly, imperfectly.

I was learning that taking a pill every day wasn't a weakness—it was taking care of myself so I could take care of my son.

I was learning that monitoring my health closely wasn't paranoia—it was responsible stewardship of the one body I have.

I was learning that accepting the reality of chronic illness didn't mean giving up—it meant living fully within new constraints.

I was also learning something else: that I couldn't keep living the way I had been. That something fundamental had to change. That the life I had built—solo parenting plus demanding career plus perfectionism plus chronic stress—was not sustainable, even with the cancer in remission.

The body was sending a clear message: Slow down. Rest. Recalibrate. Find a different way.

I heard the message. I understood it intellectually. But I didn't yet know how to act on it.

Because changing meant admitting I couldn't do it all. Changing meant letting go of the identity I had built over decades. Changing meant facing the fears that drove my perfectionism: that I wasn't enough, that I didn't belong, that if I stopped proving myself I would be revealed as inadequate.

So I kept going. Managing cancer. Managing parenting. Managing the career. Managing everything except the underlying pattern that was slowly destroying me.

The cracks were no longer hairline fractures. They were becoming chasms. The foundation was crumbling in ways that couldn't be ignored much longer.

The breaking point was approaching. But I still couldn't see it. Or perhaps I could see it but couldn't imagine an alternative, couldn't conceive of a different way of being.

The unexpected path was leading somewhere I didn't want to go but needed to reach. The transformation that would eventually emerge couldn't happen without first experiencing the complete breakdown of everything I thought I knew about strength, success, and survival.

Cancer was teaching me about limits. But I haven't finished learning yet. I would need to hit bottom before I could discover what lay beyond the relentless striving, the constant proving, the impossible standards I had set for myself.

The body had rebelled. Soon, everything else would follow.

For now, I was still standing. Still functioning. Still managing to keep all the plates spinning, even as the center began to collapse. One pill a day. One day at a time. One impossible juggling act after another. Until the day when even that wouldn't be enough anymore.

CHAPTER 9

The Breaking Point

I'm attracted to big, messy, complex problems. The kind that requires strategy, team building, organizational transformation. Things that need fixing. Things that are intellectually stimulating and exciting. Opportunities for innovation and reinvention.

These are the challenges that light me up, that make me feel alive and engaged. This is where I thrive—in the complexity, the intensity, the puzzle of making something broken work again.

The problem is that these things tend to require a degree of intensity that consumes all my energy. And with each new opportunity, with each new rung of the ladder I climbed, it became more and more apparent that this pattern would eventually lead to burnout.

More than once.

The Pattern

I get consumed with fixing the situation, solving the problem, pushing the envelope of what is possible. The intensity tugs at the fragile balance between work and self, mind and body, that I've tried so hard to create and maintain. The tension that keeps me moving forward is the same tension that holds me back, that ultimately breaks me.

I can't let go of the mission I've committed to. I can't walk away from the team I've invested in building, believing that they need me to hold things together. Even when it's destroying me.

This is the trap I kept falling into. Not just once, but repeatedly. Each time thinking I could manage it better, do it differently, avoid the collapse. Each time wrong.

The politics of organizations, when they turn toxic, destroy teams and the people on them. So I created a buffer, sheltering my staff from the toxic environment that became pervasive in multiple organizations I worked in. I absorbed the dysfunction, took the hits, and protected the team at all costs.

It took its toll.

It pulled me back into reactivity, into an earlier stage of development, into patterns I thought I had moved beyond. It didn't feel good. It didn't look good. And it wasn't good for me.

In the end, it broke me. I lost my soul in the process.

What I realized much later—years later, after significant recovery and reflection—was that the team was strong and resilient and would have weathered the storm. They didn't need me to protect them. They needed me to step aside and let them grow.

Just as a parent raising a child to adulthood must eventually let go, what they needed was for me to move on to the next challenge and let them shine in all the ways I would have wanted and expected them to. They needed me to trust them, to believe in them enough to stop buffering them from reality.

But I couldn't see that then. The middle child who had learned to mediate, to bridge differences, to hold things together—she was doing what she had always done. And it was killing her.

I could feel myself on the verge of burnout each time, but I kept pushing anyway.

The signs were always the same. Pushing myself too hard. Trying to balance the pressures of career and family. Carrying everyone else's burden on top of my own. The exhaustion that penetrated bone-deep. The inability to think clearly. The decisions that became harder and harder to make.

Burnout creeps up on you. You push it away until you can't any longer. You start to lose your focus and ability to make sound decisions. It gets harder to stay emotionally balanced. Sleep becomes elusive, and when it comes, it doesn't restore you. Negativity creeps into all aspects of life—work, relationships, your view of yourself.

You keep pushing because that's what you do. You feel the need to be there for others and deny yourself the grace of letting go of some of the burden you've been carrying around.

Each time I found myself sliding into burnout, it was harder to bounce back.

At one time, I believed I was resilient—that I could weather any kind of stress or trauma and bounce back with ease. Maybe that was true early in my career. Maybe it was true before single parenthood, before chronic illness, before the accumulated weight of years of operating at maximum capacity with no margin for error.

But repeated bouts of burnout take a deep and sustained toll—on your emotions, your psyche, your body, your spiritual being. Resilience is not infinite. It can be depleted. And with each episode, recovery becomes harder and takes longer.

The First Breaking: 2001

I can recall three distinct periods of burnout, although I imagine it was a continuous process eating away at me over years. The first was the most transformative, even if I didn't recognize it as burnout at the time.

The turmoil of massive organizational change and the personal impact it had on my career in 2001, coupled with my dad's cancer diagnosis, the loss of a long-term relationship, the upheaval of the terrorist attacks on 9/11, and eventually my dad's passing at the end of that year—all of it pushed me past burnout into something deeper. Into grief. Into a crisis of meaning.

I didn't recognize it as burnout. I thought I was just sad, just tired, just dealing with a difficult year. I needed to be there for my mom as she dealt with her grief over losing her husband of many years. So I kept pushing on despite the pain and exhaustion building inside me.

I felt empty. Hollowed out. Going through the motions of living without actually being alive.

The events of that year led me to reflect on my life and my priorities. I realized I wasn't living the life I aspired to, that there was something fundamentally missing. Losing my dad offered a window into another side of life—family—that increasingly became more important to me, more important than the career I had so carefully curated until that point.

It was this period of turmoil, burnout, grief, and reflection that ultimately led me to the most important decision I would make: to adopt a child. To enter a whole new phase of life.

The breaking led to transformation. The emptiness created space for something new to emerge.

But the pattern wasn't broken. The lessons weren't fully learned. I simply channeled the same intensity into new domains—into parenting, into advocacy, into proving I could do it all despite the added challenges.

The Second Breaking: The Federal Years

The second period of burnout emerged years later.

I was three years into my role as senior executive of a federal interagency program office, fraught with politics. It was exactly the kind of complex, messy challenge I was drawn to—trying to coordinate across agencies that had historically been in conflict, trying to build something cohesive from competing interests and entrenched positions.

I threw myself into it completely. Built a team. Created a vision. Made progress where others had failed. I was good at it. Maybe the best work of my career.

Then a new administration came in with new leaders and new ideas about how to make the persistent conflict across agencies work. Organizational transition followed. And I was pushed to the back seat.

I was forced out of the role I had given my heart and soul to. Sidelined. Stabbed in the back and thrown under the bus by colleagues and bosses—and there were many bosses, each with their own agenda. Yet I was still committed to fulfilling the promise I had made to myself and my team. This work has fulfilled my purpose. It mattered.

Increasingly, I felt diminished. Ostracized. Cast aside by those competing for position and power. I was not aligned with the new organizational direction and began to feel unmoored. I lost my purpose and eventually left the organization.

But not before absorbing months of toxicity, months of trying to protect my team, months of buffering them from the dysfunction while being slowly destroyed by it.

This all occurred during Andrei's transition from middle school into high school and then toward college. These were challenging years for both of us.

He transitioned from private school to public school—going from a school of hundreds of students to one of four thousand. I worried about his ability to thrive in a large school environment, about navigating the ins and outs of special education in a public system, about making new friends, about fitting in.

It was what he wanted, though. And over time, I realized it was what he needed. He knew, even when I didn't trust his knowledge. He quickly made friends, got involved in activities, acclimated to his new environment.

It wasn't as easy for me. Trying to advocate for him in a new system. Trying to engage with a whole new dynamic and social circle. Trying to do all of this while my professional life was falling apart.

As he was getting ready to graduate and move on to college, COVID hit.

He had just been accepted into SCAD—Savannah College of Art and Design. Our visit was cut short by the pandemic. He accepted without even seeing the school. It was a path to a career in interior design, his chosen field.

The next year was exceptionally stressful for both of us. It wasn't the normal college experience. He started college from home, online. In January 2021, at the urging of a friend, he moved to campus in Savannah into a single room and isolated for the semester.

It did not go well. He felt abandoned, uncertain, disconnected. He came home for spring quarter and finished out the year online.

All the while, my life at work continued to deteriorate.

By early summer of 2021, I made the decision to leave my federal career and launch a coaching and consulting practice. This meant abandoning the work I loved and the team I had built. I felt I had no choice. There was no place for me in the new organization—at least not one that would fulfill my intellectual and leadership desires and aspirations.

I was excluded from meetings. Minimized. Not respected for the contributions I had made and felt I could continue to make. My opinions didn't matter anymore.

At a certain point, I stopped caring. I stayed long enough to ensure my health insurance would continue when I left—still dependent on that insurance for the medication keeping me alive—and that, to the best of my ability, I would leave my team in a good place.

For the most part, I succeeded in this.

Leaving was the best thing I could have done. But I didn't realize how much stress had built up inside me and how burned out I really was.

It took a good three months for me to start to recover. A full year or more until I began to feel whole again.

I had thought I was resilient. I had thought I could bounce back quickly. The depth and duration of my depletion shocked me. This wasn't just exhaustion. This was something deeper—a fundamental depletion of my life force, my sense of purpose, my connection to myself.

The Third Breaking: Grief Upon Grief

Just as I was starting to feel like myself again, just as I was beginning to engage with life and build my coaching practice, my mom's health started to deteriorate.

Christmas 2022 would be the last Christmas together with the entire family. Christmas was a big deal in our family. We all gathered—siblings, spouses, niece and nephews—to celebrate together. It was joyous, though bittersweet. We didn't know it would be the last, but I think we sensed it.

Shortly after the holidays, Mom came down with what was likely COVID. She injured her leg, which subsequently became infected. This was the beginning of the end. She deteriorated rapidly.

In June 2023, I had just started a new consulting engagement when she was admitted to the hospital. Over the next few months, she was in and out of the hospital and rehab facilities, her health continuing to decline.

By August, she was discharged from rehab—prematurely, I believe—back home with a home health aide. I traveled back and forth between Virginia and Connecticut every few weeks to spend time with her while trying to support my new client and attempting to provide Andrei with the support he needed as he entered his final capstone year of college, which was quite intense.

I had also joined the board of directors of a nonprofit at the beginning of that year and was charged with planning a strategy offsite for the board in September, and recruiting a new CEO for the organization.

Needless to say, I was maxed out. I could feel my emotions start to fray. I was physically tired and beginning to lose focus. The latent physical and emotional exhaustion was pushing to the surface.

It wasn't long before burnout would take hold again.

In early October, Mom passed away.

It took an emotional toll on me far more than I had anticipated. I am an empath. I had been emotionally and psychologically with my mom on her journey over that final year. I had felt her turmoil, her pain, and in the end, her need to move on from this world.

It left me devastated. Unmoored. Not sure what to do or who I was without her.

Andrei felt her death deeply also. As his only known grandparent, he felt the loss acutely. It disrupted his focus on his schoolwork, though he refused to share this with his professors. We were both trying to function through grief, both failing in different ways.

Not only did I lose my mom, I also lost my place.

Her home—my childhood home, by the shore in Connecticut—was my respite. It was where I took shelter from life when it became too much. A place by the water to reflect and regenerate. The beach walks that had sustained me since childhood. The familiar rooms are full of memories. The sense of being held by history and love.

I lost this when I lost my mom. The house would be sold. That sanctuary was gone.

After her passing, things started to deteriorate at work. A new leader stepped in with whom I was not in sync. I was losing focus, juggling too many things, trying to deal with my own emotions and grief while trying to support Andrei in his grief over losing his grandmother and the stress of his culminating college experience.

I could recognize the signs of burnout this time. I have been here before. I knew what was happening. So I left the job.

It was the right decision. But it also felt like failure. Another job I couldn't sustain. Another commitment I couldn't fulfill. Another situation where I had to choose between my wellbeing and my work, and my work lost. The pattern was becoming impossible to ignore.

The Aftermath

Andrei finished school in the spring of 2024. We took a long vacation to Australia, which would turn out to be a fateful trip.

He fell in love with the country. Found his way to graduate school there. Found a life there, on the other side of the world, in a place where he could be himself without the weight of his history, without being defined by his learning differences, without being the adopted Russian kid in American schools.

I was happy for him. Proud of him. Terrified to lose him to a place so far away. And facing, once again, the question of who I was when not defined by being his mother, his advocate, his constant support.

I am only now beginning to emerge from the accumulation of years of stress, burnout, and grief that seem to have consumed me.

I'm not sure where I will go from here. What my purpose is. What comes next.

For someone who has always had a plan, who has always known the next goal, the next milestone, the next mountain to climb, this uncertainty is disorienting. Terrifying. And also, strangely, liberating.

Looking back, I can see the pattern clearly now, even if I couldn't see it while living it.

Each episode of burnout was preceded by the same sequence: Taking on a big, complex challenge. Throwing myself into it completely. Building a team. Making progress. Encountering organizational dysfunction or political upheaval. Trying to protect my team from the toxicity. Absorbing the stress myself. Depleting my resources. Ignoring the warning signs. Pushing through until I couldn't anymore. Breaking.

And each time, the breaking was compounded by grief.

The first time, grief over my father's death and the end of a long relationship. The second time, grief over the loss of meaningful work and professional identity. The third time, grief over my mother's death and the loss of my childhood home and sanctuary.

Burnout upon grief upon burnout upon grief. Each layer makes recovery harder, taking longer, going deeper.

I thought I was resilient. I thought resilience meant the ability to keep going, to push through, to handle whatever came. I thought my strength lay in my capacity to manage stress, to juggle multiple demands, to be everything to everyone.

But that's not resilience. That's endurance. And endurance has limits, even when we refuse to acknowledge them.

True resilience, I'm learning, includes the wisdom to know when to stop. The strength to admit you can't do it all. The courage to choose yourself even when it feels like abandoning others.

The Lessons, Hard-Won

There are lessons I've learned through these repeated breakings, though I resisted them every step of the way.

I learned that I can't protect people from growth by shielding them from difficulty. The teams I tried so hard to buffer from organizational dysfunction—they were stronger than I gave them credit for. They didn't need my protection. They needed my trust.

I learned that dedication can become self-destruction when it crosses the line from commitment to martyrdom. There's a difference between serving a mission and sacrificing yourself on its altar. I kept crossing that line, kept conflating the two, kept believing that giving everything meant I was doing the right thing.

I learned that my worth is not measured by my productivity, my achievements, or my usefulness to others. This is perhaps the hardest lesson, the one I'm still learning. The black sheep who spent her life proving she belonged, proving she was smart enough, capable enough, valuable enough—she built her entire identity on external validation through achievement.

When the achievements stopped, when the work fell away, when I could no longer perform at the level I had always maintained, who was I? What was my value?

I'm still working on answering that question.

I learned that grief and burnout create a particularly toxic combination. Each amplifies the other. The exhaustion of burnout makes it harder to process grief. The emotional depletion of grief makes it harder to recover from burnout. Together, they can take you to places you never imagined you could go—dark places, empty places, places where you lose yourself entirely.

I learned that some patterns can only be broken by hitting bottom. I couldn't think my way out of this pattern. I couldn't strategize a solution. I couldn't plan my way around it. I had to actually break—completely, undeniably—before I could begin to build something different.

I am only now—years after the first burnout, months after the latest—beginning to emerge from the accumulated damage.

I'm taking my cues from the universe and the signs that emerge when I most need them. This is new for me. Foreign. The planner, the strategist, the woman who always had the next five years mapped out—she's learning to not have all the answers, to not always have a plan.

The answers may be elusive. The plan is yet to form. And maybe that's okay. Maybe that's necessary. Maybe the constant planning and strategizing was part of the problem, part of the way I tried to control the uncontrollable and create safety through certainty.

There is wisdom in the universe, wisdom in the body, wisdom in the patterns that emerge when we stop forcing outcomes. This is what I'm learning to trust now.

It has led me to where I am. And it is the path forward, even when I can't see where that path leads.

The black sheep who always knew she had to chart her own course is discovering that sometimes the course charts itself. Sometimes the unexpected path isn't one you choose but one that chooses you, that reveals itself through a series of breakings and rebuildings, through the gradual dissolution of everything you thought you knew about strength and success and survival.

I am being rebuilt. Not back into what I was—that version is gone, broken beyond repair. Into something new, something I can't yet fully see or name.

The breaking point wasn't an ending. It was, in the most painful way possible, a beginning.

But I'm getting ahead of myself. The rebuilding comes later. For now, I'm still in the ruins, still learning what it means to be broken, still discovering what survives when everything else falls away. Still learning that the answer to "Who am I when I'm not proving myself?" is the most important question I've ever asked. Still learning that recovery is not the same as returning to what was. Still learning that sometimes you have to lose everything to find out what actually matters.

The breaking point broke me open. What comes next depends on what I do with the opening.

CHAPTER 10

Rising from the Ashes

It took about two years for me to start to emerge from the burnout and grief I was experiencing.

Two years. That's a long time to be underwater, to exist in a fog, to feel like a ghost moving through your own life.

But that's how long it took. Maybe longer, if I'm honest. The brain fog started to lift gradually, almost imperceptibly at first. I could feel my focus and energy slowly, tentatively begin to return. Like spring coming after an endless winter—not all at once, but in small signs, incremental shifts, moments of clarity breaking through the murk.

The last few years had been filled with withdrawal, reflection, and eventually—finally—a focus on healing. Burnout and grief persisted for a long period, taking a toll on my psyche that I'm still fully understanding. Depression took away my energy and interest in doing the things I loved. Not the acute depression of crisis, but the gray, numbing depression of depletion. The kind that makes everything feel pointless, that drains meaning from activities that once brought joy.

I tried to maintain the consistent patterns that had always worked for me before. Regular daily exercise—running, cycling, movement that kept me connected to my body. Getting outside into nature, walking the dog, enjoying the sunshine on nice days, wallowing in the rainy weather when it matched my internal landscape.

These practices sustained me, even when I couldn't feel their benefit. They were threads connecting me to the person I had been, anchors when everything else felt unmoored. Some days, they were the only things that got me out of bed.

The Contraction

Friends I had leaned on moved on with their lives. This is what happens when you withdraw. People can only hold space for so long before they need to tend to their own lives, their own concerns.

Being an introvert, it was hard for me in my burnout and grief to fully engage with others, even those I had been close with. In my typical fashion, I withdrew. I didn't have it in me to show up, to be present, to participate in the social rituals that friendship requires. I cancelled plans. I stopped reaching out. I let connections atrophy through benign neglect.

I knew I was doing it. I knew it was a pattern—the black sheep retreating when things get hard, the middle child who never quite felt she belonged now not even trying to belong. I couldn't muster the energy to fight it. I didn't have the capacity to maintain relationships while barely maintaining myself.

Family became more distant, although always a phone call away. The connection that had been forged through our common bond of "Mom" was gone. Without her as the organizing center, as the reason we all gathered, maintaining the sibling bond took more effort. We had lived different lives, chosen different paths. What connected us now felt more tenuous, requiring intention and energy I struggled to generate.

Things I had started just prior to Mom's passing became immensely more challenging. The nonprofit work I had been excited to engage in became just one more burden to bear. I couldn't muster the energy and focus to fully engage in the work I knew I should be doing, the work others were relying on me for.

I continued teaching and I loved working with new leaders. I had difficulty finding purpose in work I had previously loved. The consulting and coaching work that had once energized me now held less interest. I felt as though I was just going through the motions. I'm sure it was apparent that I wasn't fully present. The light had gone out. I was performing a role rather than inhabiting it.

I floundered. I wasn't getting the opportunities I knew I could deliver on. I was in a downward spiral, and I wallowed at the bottom, unable or unwilling to climb out yet.

Letting People Down

I knew I was letting a lot of people down. I knew it when it was happening, and as much as I wanted to do better, I couldn't. I didn't have the emotional, mental, and physical capacity.

I couldn't continue to give all I had to others, and it hurt me as much as it hurt them. Maybe more. Because I had built my entire identity around being capable, reliable, the one who showed up, the one who delivered, the one who didn't let people down.

And now I was failing at all of it.

The perfectionist who had spent her life proving she was good enough was confronting undeniable evidence that she wasn't good enough. Not anymore. Maybe not ever again.

This is what rock bottom looks like, I thought. This is what it feels like when all the structures you've built your life upon crumble. When the identity you've curated falls apart. When you can't be who you've always been and have no idea who else you might be.

This time, though, I knew what was happening. I recognized it as burnout, as grief, as depression. I understood it as a process, not a permanent state. I had been here before—not this deep, perhaps, but deep enough to know that it doesn't last forever, that eventually something shifts.

I told myself: Stay quiet. Let recovery happen at its own pace. Don't force it. Don't try to strategize your way out. Don't create a plan and timeline for healing.

Just be. Just wait. In time, you will come back to the world.

This was radical for someone like me—the planner, the strategist, the woman who had always had the next five years mapped out. To simply wait, to trust the process, to let go of control and allow healing to unfold in its own time.

The previous breakings had taught me something crucial: you can't think your way out of burnout. You can't strategize your way through grief. You have to feel it, endure it, allow it to transform you. You have to trust that something on the other side of the breaking exists, even when you can't see it yet.

Small Openings

I took on a few new coaching clients during this period, and something began to emerge. I began to realize that the work that inspires me—the work that penetrates the fog even when everything else feels meaningless—is helping others find their purpose and the place in which they can live their values in alignment with their work.

A mirror of myself, perhaps. What I couldn't yet do for myself, I could help others do. What I had lost —purpose, meaning, values alignment—I could help others discover or reclaim.

There was something in this work that called to me even in my depleted state. When I sat with a coaching client, when I helped them see patterns they couldn't see, when I held space for their transformation, something in me came alive. Just for an hour. Just briefly. But alive nonetheless.

These moments were breadcrumbs leading me back to myself.

Still, I wasn't sure what was next for me. I focused on the things that were important to me, the things that touched my soul, yet I wasn't sure what would fulfill my own purpose and values. I could help others find their way, but I remained lost in my own landscape.

Supporting Andrei's Journey

Much of my time and energy during this period was spent helping my son navigate post-college life and all the uncertainty that came with it.

Supporting his search for interior design jobs that didn't materialize in the saturated market. Navigating his decision to move across the world to Australia for a graduate program in interior architecture, fulfilling his dream to live and study—and hopefully work—abroad.

Helping him get settled in his new home, learning more about "down under" culture and sustainable and regenerative design than I ever imagined I would. Planning a home renovation with him—a legacy to the interior designer he had become, a tangible way to stay connected across the distance.

In some ways, focusing on his journey gave me respite from my own. I could channel the strategic thinking, the problem-solving, the planning capabilities into helping him when I couldn't yet help myself. I could be useful, valuable, needed—even if only from afar, even if only as a sounding board and source of encouragement.

And I was proud of him. So proud. He was building a life on his own terms, in his own way. The black sheep son of a black sheep mother, both of us charting unconventional paths, both of us learning that being different isn't something to fix but something to honor.

Watching him thrive gave me hope that maybe I could thrive again too. Maybe reinvention was possible at any age. Maybe the breaking point wasn't the end but a new beginning.

What Kept Me Grounded

My pets kept me anchored during this time. Although we lost our first cat, Bandit, Johnny—my precious golden retriever-husky —and playful kitten Pierre were by my side with all their love and affection.

Animals don't care about your productivity. They don't judge your worth by your achievements. They love you simply for being, for showing up, for existing in their space. When I felt worthless, when I couldn't deliver on my own expectations or anyone else's, they reminded me that being is enough.

Johnny's walks got me outside even on days when I wanted to hide inside. Pierre's antics made me laugh when I thought I'd forgotten how. Their need for care gave me structure when everything else felt formless. They kept me tethered to life when I wanted to drift away from it.

Meditation and exercise kept me centered. I continued my daily workouts, meeting new gym friends in the process—casual connections that didn't require deep engagement but reminded me that I could still connect with people, still be part of a community, even in limited ways.

Weekly and monthly meditation practice became essential. Learning and practicing the ways of Buddhism with special friends and our master from a coach training program five years earlier. These sessions offered something I desperately needed: a framework for understanding suffering, for sitting with difficulty without trying to fix it, for being present with what is rather than what should be.

Buddhism's teachings about impermanence, about the nature of suffering, about letting go of attachment—they spoke to exactly where I was. Everything is temporary. Pain is inevitable but suffering is optional. The self we cling to is an illusion. Let go. Let go. Let go.

Slowly, incrementally, these practices began to work. Chatting with neighbors while walking the dog. Neighborhood wine nights, gathering with old and new friends. Small connections, low-stakes interactions, gradual re-entry into the social world.

These threads of connection began pulling me out of the depths and silent pain of burnout and grief. Until one day, I looked in the mirror and recognized vestiges of myself. Not the person I had been—that person was gone. But glimpses of who I might become.

Reflection and Understanding

During this recovery period, I spent time reflecting on the deep introspection and personal assessments I had done throughout coach training and practice. I pulled out old journals, revisited assessments, looked at patterns that had emerged over years of self-inquiry.

Consistent characteristics appeared across all the assessments: thoughtful, creative, a strategist, innovative, seeks meaning in work, cares deeply about the well-being of others.

These weren't just descriptors. They were core aspects of who I am, constants that persisted despite the burnout, despite the grief, despite feeling lost and purposeless. They were foundation stones on which I could rebuild.

Revisiting my life journey through the lens of adult development and maturation illuminated new insights. I had studied developmental theory in my doctoral work, applied it in my consulting, yet had never fully applied it to my own journey. Vertical development occurs when meaning makes systems shift, opening the window to see the world through a new lens, building the capacity to handle ambiguity and paradox, and redefining identity.

The concept of "fallback" particularly resonated —the idea that life's challenges and environmental circumstances can develop to later stages of meaning, making identity, and engaging with the world. When we're under extreme stress, when we experience trauma or loss or overwhelming circumstances, we often fallback to earlier, less mature ways of being.

This helped me understand what had happened. The circumstances I had navigated—the accumulated burnout, the grief over my parents' deaths, the cancer, the solo parenting challenges, the organizational dysfunction—all of it had pushed me back into a trough of emotion and reaction that I thought I had moved beyond.

I had fallen back. Not because I was weak. Not because I had failed. But because the load exceeded my capacity, and the systems that usually supported more mature functioning simply collapsed under the weight.

This understanding was liberating. It meant I wasn't broken permanently. It meant the regression was temporary, a natural response to overwhelming circumstances. It meant I could develop forward again, could recover the ground I'd lost and potentially move beyond where I'd been before.

As I emerged from the depths, I began seeing the world in a new way. I could recognize when I was being pulled back into old patterns of being. The hypervigilance, the perfectionism, the need to prove myself, the drive to be indispensable, the inability to rest—I could see these patterns emerging and choose differently.

Not always. Not perfectly. More often than before.

The Enneagram Window

Exploring the Enneagram opened a window into my childhood, and later development that connected many dots I hadn't been able to connect before. I better understood motivations and behaviors established early in life. Overlaid with vertical development, the arc of my life started to make sense. I was able to connect many dots that hadn't been connected in my mind before.

I am a Tri-Type—the Individualist, the Romantic, what some call the Sensitive Maverick. A unique, creative soul who avoids being ordinary at all costs. I focus on being authentic, always seeking my true self. Emotions run deep and intense, and I value intellectual mastery and systems thinking, and drive toward big-picture integration and harmony. My self-preservation instinct is protective of energy, emotional space, identity.

Reading about Type SP Four Five Nine characteristics felt like reading my own biography written by someone who had been watching my entire life.

The sense of being fundamentally different from others. The feeling that something essential is missing. The search for identity and significance. The attraction to beauty and depth. The tendency toward melancholy and longing. The creative expression. The authenticity at all costs, the need for mastery and intellectual autonomy.

It's hard feeling so deeply and so intensely all the time. This is what I had never been able to articulate before. Why does everything hit me so hard? Why I can't just move on quickly from setbacks. Why do I absorb the emotions of others like a sponge? Why do I feel alienated even in groups where I should belong? Why I often feel misunderstood. Why do I withdraw when the system seems misaligned, constraining, non-supportive?

My type often feels that something is missing, that they're fundamentally flawed or lacking, that if they could just find that missing piece they would finally be whole, unique, and understood by others.

I'm still searching, though I'm more able to accept myself as I am. The search itself is part of who I am. My thirst for knowledge and meaning in the universe will always propel me forward. Learning to build regenerative systems isn't a problem to be solved. It's a feature of my nature.

Understanding this helped me have compassion for myself in ways I never had before. The black sheep wasn't broken. She was wired for depth, for meaning, for authenticity. She was never going to be content with surface-level success or conventional measures of achievement. She needed something more—purpose, meaning, alignment with her deepest values.

And the burnout, the breaking—these happened because I kept trying to be someone I wasn't, to succeed in systems built for different types of people, to prove my worth through achievements that didn't actually fulfill my soul's deeper needs.

The Slow Return

Recovery was not linear. There were good days and terrible days. Days when I felt like myself again and days when the fog descended and I couldn't remember why anything mattered.

But slowly, incrementally, the trajectory shifted from decline to plateau to gradual ascent. The brain fog lifted more often than it descended. The energy returned in small increments. The interest in work, in relationships, in life itself—it began to resurface, tentative at first, then with more conviction.

I started taking on more coaching clients, more selectively than before. I said no to opportunities that didn't align with my values or serve my purpose. I created boundaries I had never maintained before. I prioritized rest, recovery, reflection over productivity and achievement.

This was radical for someone who had built her identity on being busy, on delivering results, on never saying no to a challenge. But the breaking had taught me something crucial: I have limits. Everyone has limits. Ignoring those limits doesn't make you strong—it makes you unsustainable.

I began to see my past differently. Not as a series of achievements punctuated by failures, but as a journey of becoming. All of it—the striving, the achieving, the burnout, the grief, the breaking, the recovery—all of it was necessary. All of it was teaching me something essential about who I am and who I'm meant to be. This is what development looks like.

The black sheep who had spent her life trying to prove she belonged was finally understanding: belonging isn't about fitting in. It's about being fully yourself and finding the people, the work, the life that honors that fullness.

As I emerged from the ashes of burnout and grief, I wasn't the same person who had gone into them. I couldn't be. That person had been consumed by the fire.

But what emerged wasn't less. It was different. More essential. More aligned. More real.

I had less tolerance for bullshit—organizational politics, performative leadership, work that looked impressive on paper but accomplished nothing meaningful. I had lost patience for pretending, for playing roles, for being who others needed me to be.

I had more compassion—for myself, for others struggling with challenges I couldn't see, for the messy reality of being human in a world that demands perfection. I had learned that vulnerability isn't weakness, that asking for help isn't failure, that limits are real and honoring them is wisdom not inadequacy.

I had a deeper understanding—of systems and patterns, of how personal and professional are intertwined, of how our earliest experiences shape our entire lives, of how the body keeps the score and the soul demands authenticity even when it costs us everything we've built.

I had clearer priorities—purpose over prestige, alignment over achievement, being over doing, depth over breadth, quality over quantity, meaning over metrics.

I had stronger boundaries—around time, energy, commitment, availability. I had learned the hard way that saying yes to everything means saying no to yourself, and that eventually the self will extract payment for being neglected.

I still didn't know exactly where I was going. I still didn't have a five-year plan or clear career trajectory. I still woke up some days uncertain about my purpose, my path, my next steps.

But I had something more valuable: the willingness to not know. The capacity to sit with uncertainty. The trust that the path would reveal itself in its own time. The faith that who I'm becoming is more important than what I'm achieving.

The Phoenix Rises

They say the phoenix rises from its own ashes, reborn and renewed. It's a powerful metaphor, one that captures something essential about transformation.

But what the metaphor doesn't capture is how long it takes for the ashes to cool. How painful the burning is. How disorienting it is to be remade. How you lose everything familiar, everything you relied on for identity and security, before you can become something new.

And how what rises from the ashes isn't the same bird that went into the fire. It looks different. It sounds different. It flies differently. It is fundamentally, irreversibly changed.

I was rising from the ashes. Slowly. Imperfectly. With many setbacks and stumbles. But rising nonetheless. The woman who emerged from the burnout and grief wasn't the strategic consultant who climbed the corporate ladder. She wasn't the perfectionist who demanded excellence from herself and everyone around her. She wasn't the solo mother holding everything together through sheer force of will. She wasn't the cancer patient fighting to survive. She wasn't the advocate battling systems that didn't work.

She was all of those things and none of them. She carried those experiences as part of her story, but they no longer defined her completely. She had been broken down to something more essential, more fundamental, more true.

And from that essential truth, something new was beginning to grow. What exactly? I'm still discovering. Still becoming. Still allowing the emergence of whoever I'm meant to be next. But this much I know: I am rising. Changed. Scarred. Uncertain. But rising.

And in the rising, I am finally, truly, becoming myself.

The unexpected path had taken me through fire. Now I was learning to fly with whatever wings emerged from the burning. The journey wasn't over. It was just beginning again. But this time, I was beginning from a different place. From the ashes. From the truth. From the essential core that survived when everything else burned away.

This time, I was beginning.

CHAPTER 11

The Coaching Calling

Coaching called me long before I became a practicing coach.

I can see that now, looking back. The threads were there throughout my entire journey—the fascination with how people develop, the desire to help others grow, the questions about what makes great leaders great, the orientation toward service rather than power. All of it was pointing toward coaching, even when I couldn't yet see where it was leading.

But at the time, I had no idea this path existed, no concept that there was a profession dedicated to helping leaders become more effective, more authentic, more aligned with their deepest values and highest potential.

The path to coaching began, as so many important journeys do, by accident.

The Introduction

I was introduced to coaching through a leadership development program hosted by my employer. New to the company, I was focused on building my team, engaging with clients, architecting strategy for the group, and integrating into the organization.

When I had the opportunity to join the inaugural cohort of this program, I jumped at the chance. Not only did it reflect confidence in me as a leader, it gave me the opportunity to build new skills and competencies and associate with leaders outside my day-to-day work.

I immersed myself in the program and the burgeoning literature in the field of leadership. Although I had extensive academic and professional experience in management, I had not previously considered leadership competencies as distinct from management.

This distinction was revelatory.

Management is about systems, processes, efficiency, execution. Leadership is about vision, inspiration, transformation, development. Management asks "How do we do this right?" Leadership asks "What is the right thing to do?" Management optimizes existing systems. Leadership creates new possibilities.

I had been managing people and projects for years. But had I been leading?

My eyes were opened to what it means to be a leader—not in title or position, but in actual practice. What does it mean to develop people rather than simply directing them? What does it mean to create conditions for others to thrive rather than simply extracting performance? What does it mean to lead with authenticity and vulnerability rather than armor and control?

As is typical for me, I jumped in with both feet. I was enamored with what I was learning about leadership, leader development, and the things that make great leaders great. I was fascinated with the world of psychometric assessments—leadership styles, personality preferences, work styles—and how they influence how a leader engages and leads.

I threw myself into the deep personal work of becoming an effective leader. I collaborated with a coach as I worked to discover the authentic leader in me while taking on a stretch assignment designed to build the leadership competencies that aligned with that authentic self.

This was different from anything I had done before. The doctoral work had been intellectually rigorous but not personally transformative. This was both. I was learning theories and frameworks, but I was also doing the inner work—examining my motivations, confronting my shadows, challenging my assumptions about what leadership required.

And I was working with a coach who held space for that development in ways I had never experienced. Someone who asked questions rather than providing answers. Someone who believed in my capacity to find my own way rather than telling me what to do. Someone who reflected back to me patterns I couldn't see in myself.

The experience planted a seed: Maybe this is what I'm meant to do. Maybe helping others develop as leaders is where my skills, my experience, my orientation toward service, all converge. I had begun to incorporate coaching into how I lead my teams - leader as coach. Was there more though?

The Shift

Circumstances evolved, and I left that company for a leadership position in a not-for-profit research and consulting firm. I was drawn to serving others and believed such an organization would fulfill that purpose for me.

The reality was quite different, and my tenure with the company wasn't long. The mission was noble, but the internal dynamics were toxic. Another lesson in the gap between espoused values and lived values, between organizational aspiration and reality.

It was during this time that a former colleague enrolled in one of the premier leadership coaching programs—Georgetown University's Leadership Coaching program. She talked about it with such enthusiasm, such energy, such sense of having found her calling.

It wasn't long before I followed suit.

I was feeling disenfranchised with the competitive realities of the professional services business. I was tired of the politics, the posturing, the focus on revenue over impact. I sought a role that would be better suited to my service orientation and desire to help others.

Coaching became my calling.

The Transformation

The Leadership Coaching program at Georgetown was life-changing. Not only did I have the opportunity to learn from the leaders in the field of coaching, my colleagues in my cohort were of like mind—many seeking purpose, many seeking a new start, as I was.

We were doctors and lawyers and corporate executives and nonprofit leaders, all of us sensing that something was missing from our professional lives, all of us drawn to this work of helping others develop and transform.

Being a great coach requires a deep understanding of oneself. This is what I learned first and most importantly. You can't take someone else deeper than you've gone yourself. You can't help others confront their shadows if you haven't confronted your own. You can't hold space for another's transformation if you haven't experienced your own.

The program involved deep introspective work. Delving into motivations, shadows, fears, life stories. Discovering the dark side while illuminating the bright side. Reflecting on what drivers might be holding me back from pursuing what I was discovering as my purpose in serving others.

I examined my need to be seen as competent, my fear of being revealed as inadequate, my drive to prove myself through achievement. I explored my tendency to take on too much, to buffer others from difficulty, to sacrifice myself in service of team or mission. I confronted my perfectionism and the ways it limited both my own growth and my ability to support others' growth.

This was uncomfortable work. There were sessions where I cried. Sessions where I wanted to quit. Sessions where I felt exposed in ways that terrified me.

But there were also moments of profound clarity. Moments where patterns I had lived for decades suddenly became visible. Moments where I understood, finally, why I made the choices I made, why I struggled in the ways I struggled, why certain situations triggered me while others didn't.

We learned the tools and techniques of the coaching trade: active listening, asking powerful open-ended questions, practicing appreciative inquiry, giving feedback, goal setting and calls to action.

We learned to coach the person, not their issues. To work with their values and beliefs, their ladder of inference, their wheel of life. To use leadership, personality, and work style assessments not as diagnostic tools but as conversation starters, as mirrors for reflection.

We learned about approaching leadership with a beginner's mindset, about progressing through the competency cycle from unconscious incompetence to unconscious competence. About recognizing how thoughts, feelings, and actions interact as a leader. About effective communication and decision-making.

We practiced mindfulness and self-care, meditation, somatic work to stay grounded and centered. We studied the path of adult development and leadership maturity—the very frameworks I would later use to understand my own journey through burnout and recovery.

And we practiced coaching. Hours and hours of practice with each other, with volunteer clients, in triads where one person coached, one was coached, and one observed. Learning to sit with silence. Learning to resist the urge to solve problems or give advice. Learning to trust the client's own wisdom and capacity.

This was harder than it sounds. For someone who had built her career on being smart, on having answers, on solving complex problems, learning to simply be present without fixing anything was profoundly challenging.

But it was also liberating. To realize that my value didn't lie in having all the answers. To discover that asking good questions is often more powerful than providing solutions. To experience how people flourish when given space and support rather than direction and control.

The work connected everything I had learned and experienced. My systems thinking helped me see patterns and connections clients couldn't see. My strategic mind helped me ask questions that opened new possibilities. My empathy helped me attune to what wasn't being said. My own struggles helped me hold space for others' struggles without judgment or fear.

All of it—the doctoral work, the consulting, the leadership roles, the solo parenting, the special education advocacy, the burnout, the grief—all of it was preparation for this work. All of it gave me capacity and wisdom I could now use in service of others' development.

It was an overwhelming and transformative experience. It left me with new knowledge and tools and a potential new path forward. I felt prepared as a coach, yet in my ongoing desire for mastery, it would take time to gain confidence to fully engage in the practice of coaching.

The Practical Barriers

While I entertained thoughts of launching a coaching practice at the end of the program, I was faced with the reality of childcare, health insurance, tutors, therapies, and school tuition.

The practical part of me couldn't get past the fear of launching into the unknown. How would I replace my salary? How would I maintain health insurance—crucial given my chronic illness and daily medication? How would I pay for Andrei's specialized education? What if I couldn't build a client base quickly enough? What if I failed?

So I waited.

While engaged in full-time health policy and IT work, I tried to build a coaching practice on the side. With little disposable time, it was unrealistic. I didn't have the bandwidth. Solo parenting, demanding job, chronic illness, special education advocacy—there was no space for launching a new practice, no energy for the marketing and networking required to build a client base.

I settled for continuing education to build my skills and competencies as a coach—learning more about coaching methods, techniques, and leadership assessment tools. I invested in the things that had caught my interest: team coaching, vertical development, leadership maturity. I became certified in assessment tools like the Leadership Circle Profile, the Hogan assessment, and EQ-i 2.0, an emotional intelligence assessment.

I was preparing for something, even if I couldn't yet fully commit to it. Building skills and credentials for a future I could envision but not yet inhabit.

The black sheep, once again preparing for a path that didn't yet exist, that would require leaving safety behind, that would demand a leap of faith.

It wasn't enough to quell my desire to move beyond the constraining leadership position I was in and into a role that allowed me to continue growing as a coach and leadership development professional.

Coaching was calling me, and the political environment in my current position was pushing me out. The organizational dysfunction, the backstabbing, the misalignment with new leadership—it was all becoming untenable.

In a heart-wrenching move, I made the break. Left the government position. Once again I hung out my shingle as a consultant and a coach.

This was 2021, in the midst of recovering from the second major burnout, during COVID, as Andrei was struggling with remote college. The timing was terrible. But the alternative—staying in a toxic situation that was destroying me—was worse.

It wasn't as easy as I thought it would be. I was burned out from the politics, posturing, and stress of trying to salvage the interagency work and team I was so committed to. I was depleted in ways I didn't fully recognize yet.

I became certified as an Associate Certified Coach (ACC) with the International Coaching Federation and began to professionally transition from health IT professional and government leader to coach. I had to remake and market myself as something different than what most people in my professional network associated me with.

It took time and energy that was in short supply. I aligned with multiple coaching platforms and leaned on trusted colleagues for references and referrals. Gradually, things started to take shape, and I was on the road to building a successful practice as a leadership and executive coach.

But then my mother got sick. Then she died. Then I fell into the third and deepest burnout, the one that would take two years to emerge from.

The coaching practice continued, but I couldn't show up for it the way I wanted to, the way my clients deserved. I was going through the motions, performing a role rather than fully inhabiting it. Some clients stayed with me through it. Others, sensing my absence, moved on. I don't blame them.

The Integration

The path to becoming a coach was a lifelong endeavor. It wasn't something I decided to do and then did. It was the accumulation of years of experience, education, training, practice, and deep introspection about who I am and who I want to be as a person, as a coach, and as a leader in service to others.

The choices, challenges, and crossroads along the way made me who I am.

The black sheep childhood taught me to see differently, to question conventional wisdom, to trust my own perception even when it differed from others'.

The doctoral work gave me frameworks for understanding complex systems and human behavior.

The consulting career taught me about strategy, about organizational dynamics, about the gap between what leaders say and what they do.

The adoption taught me about vulnerability, about leading with heart rather than only with head, about service that costs you everything.

The special education journey taught me about advocacy, about seeing strengths in what others label as deficits, about honoring different ways of being in the world.

The cancer taught me about limits, about mortality, about what actually matters when you're facing uncertainty.

The burnout taught me about the price of perfectionism, about the difference between dedication and self-destruction, about the necessity of choosing yourself sometimes.

The grief taught me about loss, about impermanence, about the depth of love revealed only through its absence.

All of it—every struggle, every achievement, every breaking, every recovery—prepared me to sit with others in their own struggles, to hold space for their development, to ask questions that help them see what they couldn't see before, to trust their capacity to find their own way.

I've learned to trust my intuition, to lead with my heart, and to rely on my mind and body as foundational guideposts. These aren't just coaching principles. They're life principles, hard-won through decades of experience and reflection.

The work I do now as a coach isn't separate from who I am. It's an expression of who I am, the integration of all I've learned and all I've become. When I sit with a client, I bring my whole self—the strategist and the empath, the systems thinker and the intuitive, the intellectual and the emotional, the person who has succeeded and the person who has failed, the leader who has achieved and the person who has broken completely.

This integration is what makes me effective as a coach. Not my credentials, not my frameworks, not my tools and techniques—though all of these matter. What matters most is my capacity to be present, to see, to understand, to hold space, to believe in possibility even when the person I'm coaching can't yet believe it themselves.

A New Calling

It's not the end of my journey. A new calling is emerging.

I can feel it the way I felt coaching calling me before I had language for it. A pull toward something I can't yet fully articulate. A sense that there's another layer of development, another transformation waiting.

What is it? I'm not entirely sure yet.

Perhaps it's about working at a larger scale—not just with individual leaders but with systems and organizations. Perhaps it's about teaching and mentoring other coaches. Perhaps it's about writing and speaking, sharing the hard-won wisdom in ways that reach beyond one-on-one coaching relationships.

Perhaps it's about integration at an even deeper level—bringing together leadership development, systems change, personal transformation, and collective evolution in ways I can't yet envision.

Or perhaps it's about something I can't even imagine yet, something that will reveal itself only as I continue to walk this unexpected path.

What I know is this: I'm not forcing it. I'm not strategizing it. I'm not planning it out in meticulous detail the way I once would have.

I'm listening. Noticing. Paying attention to what calls me, what energizes me, what feels aligned with my deepest values and highest purpose.

I'm trusting the process. The same process that led me from engineering and healthcare management to doctoral work to consulting to adoption to coaching. The same process that broke me down and rebuilt me. The same process that is always, always leading me toward more authentic expression of who I'm meant to be.

The black sheep who spent her life trying to prove she belonged has finally understood:

belonging isn't about conforming. It's about becoming so fully yourself that you create space for others to do the same.

The coach who helps others find their path is still discovering her own path. And that's exactly as it should be. We're all works in progress, all becoming, all learning, all growing.

The coaching calling wasn't the end of the journey. It was another beginning.

And whatever comes next—whatever new calling is emerging—I'm ready for it. Not because I have all the answers or because I've figured it all out. But because I've learned to walk into uncertainty with openness, to trust emergence, to believe that the path will reveal itself when I need it to.

The unexpected path continues. And I continue to walk it, one step at a time, one transformation at a time, one integration at a time.

Becoming, always becoming, who I'm meant to be.

The calling called me. And I answered.

Now I'm listening for the next call, the next evolution, the next becoming.

And trusting that when it comes, I'll recognize it. Because this is what the entire journey has been preparing me for: the capacity to hear the call, the courage to answer, and the wisdom to know that every ending is also a beginning.

The coach is still being coached by life itself. And the lessons continue.

CHAPTER 12

Connected Wisdom

I've come full circle on my hero's journey.

In Joseph Campbell's archetypal story, the hero leaves their ordinary world to follow a calling, encounters the unknown, tests their will in foreign lands, and returns home with newfound knowledge and wisdom that they impart to their community.

I set out on my journey as a young, idealistic professional, not sure what life would hold but certain that I wanted to matter. I wanted to "do good" and change the world, fulfilling goals yet to be defined. I sought knowledge and mastery in fields that piqued my interest. My interests were broad and deep—fascinated by science, the human body, the natural world, psychology and psyche, organizational dynamics. I was awed by the functional complexity of humans and organizations as systems, by the elements in the natural world, by the complexity and interconnectedness of the universe and our place in it.

The black sheep who felt different, who never quite fit, was driven to understand—herself, others, systems, the world. The quest for understanding became the organizing principle of her life.

My path led me to the intersection of policy, management, technology, and healthcare. Later, I discovered the field of leadership as a discipline and practice, and the burgeoning field of leadership coaching. It was a next-level awareness for me of what drives us as humans, the motivations and behaviors that guide us in our interactions with others and ourselves.

It connected my intellectual passion for strategy and organizational dynamics with the role that leaders play in motivating others to fully engage as individuals and teams, creating high-performing organizations. It spoke to my desire to help others and improve the world around us. It gave me insight into the things that bring out the best we have to offer—to ourselves, to others, to the world.

The journey wasn't linear. It was circuitous, full of detours and dead ends, breakthroughs and breakdowns. But looking back, I can see how each experience, each challenge, each seeming failure was preparing me for what came next, building capacities I would desperately need, teaching lessons I could learn no other way.

Encountering the Unknown

Through my experiences as a young female professional cutting her teeth in male-dominant organizations, I encountered glass ceilings and biases toward women in management and leadership. I forged ahead regardless, believing that hard work and performance would matter, that competence and excellence would overcome bias.

My natural desire to learn and grow, to explore and test boundaries, to become expert and master new things kept me going. I continued my education, attaining a doctoral level that I hadn't always considered yet that seemed natural given my nature—the quest for knowledge, the drive for mastery, the need to prove myself through achievement.

At the same time, the roadblocks I encountered along the way became points of frustration, discouragement, doubt, and disillusionment. Biases persisted. My experience showed me that knowledge, expertise, experience, and hard work don't always matter. Politics mattered. Relationships mattered. Fitting the mold mattered. And I didn't fit the mold.

I navigated acquisitions, mergers, job changes, experimentation, and entrepreneurship. I continued to push boundaries, to challenge conventional wisdom, to chart my own course. In spite of my successes—and there were many—I began to question my choices. I wondered what I might be missing by focusing on my career at the expense of personal relationships and family.

The black sheep was succeeding on her own terms but still feeling that something essential was missing.

Circumstances would lead me to choose motherhood later in life, taking on the challenge alone. It seemed fitting. Who better than the independent woman who had weathered personal and professional challenges to take on solo parenting?

What I didn't know then was that parenthood would transform me more profoundly than any other experience in my life.

Being a parent is the hardest job in the world. It is complex—emotionally, psychologically, and physically challenging. And it brings the greatest joy one can imagine. The love of a parent for a child defies description. It can only be felt.

My life became a before-and-after picture: before adopting my son and after. Priorities shifted. Work still mattered; it just mattered differently. I strove for balance between two lives, the professional and the parent. I sought a way to be a complete person, integrating identities that had felt separate, competing, irreconcilable.

It is a journey and still a work in progress.

Along the way, I became passionate about leadership and the opportunities that leader development and coaching opens for leaders, parents, and families. I consumed everything I could—books, blogs, classes, certifications—becoming the parent, leader, coach, and writer that I am.

I evolved from expert to achiever, from socialized to self-authoring, pushing the boundaries from conventional to post-conventional stages of development. I saw the world through increasingly complex lenses. I understood systems and patterns that had been invisible before. I developed capacities for holding paradox, for navigating complexity, for leading through emergence rather than control.

The Descent

But then I fell back. The tensions between my personal development and those of the organizational systems I was part of emerged and eventually crushed me. Things no longer worked. I was no longer in sync—with the leaders, with colleagues, with the practices and values showing up.

I moved on. It was one of the hardest things I've ever done. Still committed to the mission, purpose, and people, I had to let go—for myself and my family.

I only had an inkling of the toll the persistent chronic stress would take on my physical, mental, and emotional wellbeing. It led to chronic illness—cancer cells proliferating in my bone marrow, a daily reminder that the body keeps score. It led to burnout—not once but repeatedly, each time deeper and more devastating.

And eventually, to recovery and reinvention.

This was the descent into the underworld that every hero's journey requires. The breaking down of everything I thought I knew, everything I had built my identity upon, everything that had defined success and worth and belonging.

I had to lose it all to discover what actually mattered. I had to break completely to be rebuilt differently. I had to descend into the darkness to understand what the light was for.

The Return with Wisdom

What I learned about myself on this journey is that what set me apart as a leader was my desire to put others first, in service to mission and purpose. I never aspired to position or power. I don't need the spotlight, preferring to foster the development of others in pursuit of organizational goals.

This is not the norm in most organizations, where competition for position and power in the executive echelons is intense and not for the faint of heart. My leadership style was not understood or valued, and certainly not promoted. Disillusionment set in, thrusting me into a search for meaning in my work and eventually to creating a new path as a coach, consultant, and teacher.

What I thought was a failure of leadership—my inability to compete for position and power—was actually my greatest strength as a leader. I was practicing servant leadership before I had language for it. I was leading from a more developed stage than the systems I was operating within could accommodate.

The black sheep who never fit wasn't broken. She was simply ahead of the curve, operating from a different paradigm, seeing possibilities that others couldn't yet see.

This is what I now understand about leadership: it's not about position or power or control. It's about service. It's about creating conditions for others to grow, to thrive, to become their best selves. It's about holding space for transformation while trusting the process of development. It's about seeing people not as they are but as they're capable of becoming, and believing in that potential even when they can't yet see it themselves.

Leadership is not separate from who you are. It's an expression of who you are—your values, your development, your way of being in the world. The most effective leaders are those who have done their own inner work, who know themselves deeply, who can hold complexity and paradox, who lead from authenticity rather than from armor.

This is what all my experiences taught me. This is the wisdom I now offer to the leaders I coach, to the students I teach, to anyone willing to do the hard work of becoming a more conscious, capable, compassionate leader.

The Web of Connection

There are many people who influenced me over the course of my life, my career, and my parenthood journey.

First and foremost are my parents, who were my North Star, guiding my early development and setting me on the course of independence that became my hallmark. They taught me to value education, to ask questions, to think critically, to build a life of meaning. They gave me roots even as they encouraged me to develop wings.

My siblings, different in so many ways from me and each other, connected through family history, genetics, and the experiences of childhood and growing up together. The dynamics between us—the comparisons, the competition, the need to differentiate—shaped who I became as profoundly as anything else.

My college roommates, friends to this day, who knew me when I was still becoming, who accepted me in all my quirky intensity.

My career experiences, along with my doctoral work and later immersion into leadership, had a profound effect on me. Each job brought with it soulmates, each treasured for the connections that emerged and continued through life, even if only through a heartfelt holiday card. The knowledge I gained through my health policy, strategy, and leadership work stimulated a passion for lifelong learning and illuminated the connectedness of seemingly disparate relationships, fields of study, and communities.

My studies of leadership, human development, and science-related subjects connected many dots for me. My life trajectory started to make sense. A new lens opened through which I viewed my world, my life, and my being. So many patterns of behavior and thought that had influenced me throughout my life became clear.

I began to understand how we develop as humans and as leaders, the stages of development that influence and are influenced by how we live our lives, how the choices we make and the paths we follow define us. I came to appreciate growing awareness of my developing self and embraced the freedom that comes with letting go of the need to control the future and live in the present, comfortable that the universe will guide us on the path we're supposed to be on.

And my son, Andrey—the unexpected gift, the uninvited teacher, the mirror that reflected back everything I needed to learn about love, about service, about letting go of control, about honoring differences, about showing up even when you don't know how.

The black sheep mother raising the black sheep son, both of us learning that being different is not a problem to be solved but a gift to be honored.

Strategy and Emergence

In strategy, there are different philosophies and approaches to how strategy is made. Is it top-down, with the strategy articulated by leaders at the top? Or does it emerge through the actions, behaviors, and decisions made by those doing the work? Or somewhere in between?

I spent years as a strategist believing that the answer was planning—meticulous analysis, clear goals, detailed roadmaps. If you could just think through all the variables, anticipate all the challenges, create a comprehensive plan, you could control the outcomes.

Life taught me differently.

Life is like a strategy. We have a plan for what we want our life to look like. We set goals. Develop action plans. Spend most of our lives trying to achieve the things we've set out to achieve or what others have told us we should achieve.

At some point, we realize that success isn't necessarily found in the position, money, or material things we've accumulated along the way. At some point, we understand that the plan was always provisional, that emergence matters more than planning, that being matters more than doing, that who we're becoming is more important than what we're achieving.

Like waves at the beach, life ebbs and flows like the tides lapping the shore. What you choose matters, although not as much as you think. What you do and how you do it matters more. And although we often feel compelled to "stay the course" on the path we chose, we can change direction. At any time, if our path does not suit us.

This is often the hard part—giving ourselves permission to change course, to admit the plan isn't working, to trust that another path exists even when we can't yet see it.

The wisdom I've gained is this: hold your plans lightly. Set intentions rather than rigid goals. Create space for emergence. Trust the process. Pay attention to what calls you, what energizes you, what aligns with your deepest values. Follow that, even when it makes no logical sense, even when it means abandoning the carefully constructed plans, even when others don't understand.

The path will reveal itself when you need it to. Not before. Not according to your timeline. But in its own time, in its own way.

This is the paradox of planning and emergence: you need both. You need enough structure to move forward, enough vision to know your general direction. But you also need flexibility to adjust, openness to what emerges, willingness to follow the unexpected turns.

The strategist learned to trust emergence. The planner learned to embrace uncertainty. The woman who needed to control everything learned to let go.

Becoming and Being

We are not the same person throughout our lives.

We may hold the same name, live in the same place, be part of the same community. But we are not constant, as much as we may fight change. Our experiences, associations, and learnings all influence who we are and who we become. We develop through stages, each one more complex than the last, each one offering new ways of making meaning, new capacities for holding paradoxes and navigating complexity.

Sometimes we progress forward. Sometimes we fall back. Sometimes we plateau. All of this is natural, expected, part of the human journey.

I am not who I was at twenty-five, climbing the career ladder with something to prove. I am not who I was at forty, adopting a child against all conventional wisdom. I am not who I was at fifty, burning out from the impossible load I was carrying. I am not even who I was at fifty-five, emerging from the ashes of burnout and grief.

I am who I am now, in this moment, carrying all those previous selves within me while also transcending them. Becoming, always becoming, who I'm meant to be next.

When I stepped off the treadmill long enough to look around, I saw a life of purpose, of kindness, of humility, of service. I learned how to be a better leader through parenting. I learned how to be a better parent through leadership. The two domains that had felt so separate, so in conflict, were actually teaching me the same lessons, building the same capacities, calling forth the same authentic self.

Over time, I learned to embrace uncertainty. I came to believe that there is wisdom in the universe and that if I stepped back from my need to know, to drive, to control my life, and was quiet and observant, the path would emerge.

This is perhaps the most important lesson, the one I'm still learning: trust. Trust the process. Trust the journey. Trust that you're exactly where you need to be, learning exactly what you need to learn, becoming exactly who you need to become.

The black sheep who spent her life trying to figure it all out finally learned that you can't figure it all out. You can only show up, pay attention, and trust that the path will reveal itself.

Connected Wisdom

The title of this chapter—Connected Wisdom—points to what I've come to understand as the essence of mature leadership and human development.

We are not separate. We are interconnected—with each other, with systems, with the natural world, with something larger than ourselves that we might call spirit or universe or collective consciousness.

What happens to one affects all. What we do matters, not just for ourselves but for everyone and everything we touch. Our development is not just personal—it's relational, systemic, collective.

Leadership, at its highest expression, understands this interconnection. It sees the system, not just the parts. It considers impact on all stakeholders, not just shareholders. It serves the whole, not just the self.

Wisdom comes from recognizing patterns, seeing connections, understanding how things work together. It comes from experience and reflection, from making mistakes and learning from them, from breaking down and rebuilding differently.

Connected wisdom is wisdom that holds the paradoxes:

- Planning and emergence
- Structure and flexibility
- Strength and vulnerability
- Serving and leading
- Knowing and not-knowing
- Being and becoming
- Individual and collective
- Thinking and feeling
- Achievement and being
- Holding on and letting go

It's wisdom that understands that both sides of these paradoxes are true, that we need both, that mature leadership requires the capacity to hold both simultaneously without collapsing into either/or thinking.

This is what the journey taught me. This is what the breaking opened up. This is what emerged from the ashes of burnout and grief and loss.

Not answers. Not certainty. Not a new plan.

But a different way of being. A more spacious consciousness. A capacity for holding complexity and paradox. A trust in emergence. A commitment to service. An understanding of interconnection, guided by the four immeasurables - equanimity, loving kindness, compassion and joy.

The Crossroads

I find myself here, now, again at a crossroads. Which path will I take?

The truth is, I don't know yet. And for perhaps the first time in my life, I'm okay with not knowing.

The strategist who always had a plan has learned to wait for the plan to reveal itself. The achiever who needed goals has learned to set intentions and trust the process. The perfectionist who feared being revealed as not-enough has learned that being enough doesn't require proving anything.

I know some things. I know I'm called to serve. I know coaching and teaching and writing are part of my path. I know helping leaders develop, helping systems evolve toward health, helping people find alignment between their deepest values and their work—these matter to me more than position or prestige or conventional success.

I know that whatever comes next needs to honor all of who I am—the strategist and the intuitive, the intellectual and the emotional, the planner and the mystic, the person who has succeeded and the person who has failed and learned more from the failing.

I know that I'm being called toward something larger than individual coaching, something about working at the level of systems and collective development. But I don't yet know what form that takes.

And that's okay. The not-knowing is part of it. The uncertainty is where possibility lives. The space between what was and what will be is where transformation happens.

Viktor Frankl wrote: "Between stimulus and response lives the freedom to choose."

This is where I live now—in that space of freedom between what happens and how I respond. In the choice to meet whatever comes with openness rather than armor, with curiosity rather than control, with trust rather than fear.

The black sheep who spent her life proving she belonged finally understands: belonging comes from being fully yourself, not from conforming to others' expectations. Strength comes from vulnerability, not from never breaking. Wisdom comes from not-knowing, not from having all the answers. Leadership comes from service, not from power.

The hero has completed the journey and returned with gifts: not certainty or solutions or a new plan, but something more valuable—a way of being that can hold complexity, navigate emergence, serve authentically, lead consciously.

The journey continues. It always continues. But I'm walking it differently now—with more grace, more trust, more openness to what wants to emerge.

The unexpected path brought me here. And here, I discover, is exactly where I needed to be all along.

The connected wisdom I offer is this: Trust your journey. Honor your differences. Do the inner work. Embrace the breaking—it's where transformation happens. Let go of control. Serve something larger than yourself. Pay attention to what calls you. Follow it, even when it makes no sense.

You are not broken. You are becoming. And what you're becoming is exactly what the world needs.

The black sheep was never meant to follow the flock. She was meant to forge a new path, to see what others couldn't see, to lead by being authentically herself.

And so, dear reader, are you. Your journey is your own. Your path is unique. Your gifts are needed. The wisdom is already within you. The path is already unfolding. Trust it. Trust yourself. Trust the process. And when you arrive at your own crossroads, remember: the freedom lives in the space between stimulus and response. In that space, you choose. And in that choosing, you become.

This is the wisdom. This is the journey. This is the path. And it continues, always continues, becoming and unfolding, one choice at a time, one step at a time, one transformation at a time.

The story doesn't end here. It opens. Where it leads next—for me, for you, for all of us walking this unexpected path—remains to be discovered.

And that is exactly as it should be.

www.ingramcontent.com/pod-product-compliance
Lightning Source LLC
LaVergne TN
LVHW091138080826
845145LV00008B/2195

* 9 7 8 1 9 6 9 8 2 6 5 7 3 *